Deborah
Be blessed to
go forward
Mary Hatcher
2010

Leaders:
Get Up Off The Canvas

Leaders:
Get Up Off The Canvas

Mary Holt Ashley

Copyright © 2009 by Mary Holt Ashley.

Library of Congress Control Number: 2009905213
ISBN: Hardcover   978-1-4415-3998-4
               Softcover   978-1-4415-3997-7

All rights reserved. No part of this book may be reproduced or transmitted in any form or by any means, electronic or mechanical, including photocopying, recording, or by any information storage and retrieval system, without permission in writing from the copyright owner.

This book was printed in the United States of America.

To order additional copies of this book, contact:
Xlibris Corporation
1-888-795-4274
www.Xlibris.com
Orders@Xlibris.com
59413

CONTENTS

Acknowledgement 7
Introduction 11

Chapter 1:   Mind over Matter 15
Chapter 2   Unintentional Foundation for Leadership 20
Chapter 3   Training Camp 52
Chapter 4   Featherweight 56
Chapter 5   Featherweight Champion 62
Chapter 6   Super Featherweight Champion 68
Chapter 7   Middleweight Champion 80
Chapter 8   Super Middleweight Champion 96
Chapter 9   Light Heavyweight Champion 122
Chapter 10   Middle Heavyweight Champion 132
Chapter 11   Super Heavyweight Champion 146
Chapter 12   Retirement from the Ring 160

Leadership Points for Getting up off the Canvas 167
Appendix I 169
Appendix II 172
Appendix III 174

ACKNOWLEDGEMENT

THIS BOOK IS dedicated to all of my family and especially to Ellis my husband, Chucky my son, Tekesha my daughter-in-law and Caylee Edmund my god-daughter.

The words of William A. Ward so eloquently describe my steps to completing this book: Plan purposely, prepare prayerfully, proceed positively and pursue persistently. Accomplishing this feat was one of the proudest moments in my life. Thanks be to God my dream materialized. I recognize that there are many people who played significant and equal roles in the process. Each contribution was necessary in the production process.

My parents Eddie "Buster" Holt Sr. and Ella Mae Holt who are deceased left an indelible foundation of spiritual strength, home spun values and steadfast tenacity that gave the dexterity to overcome adversity and achieve my goals. Daddy's uncanny sense of humor and mama's rich spiritual wisdom created the mold for me to get up off the canvas.

Procrastination can thwart your intentions if you are not fortunate to have a friend like Ina Watson who said to me "I am going to keep bugging you until you get started on that book and get it done." Persistently, Ina called me frequently and encouraged me to get going. She bought other author's books to show me that my story was worth writing about. She stayed on the journey and when my juices got going she celebrated each step of the way. Ina many thanks for your unwavering support.

As I got more chapters written it was difficult for me to remember whether I had written a particular piece or was it in my head. Ruth Franklin a friend and colleague offered to read the chapters. A very time consuming task but she so superbly and patiently provided input about the chapters. Ruth thanks for the many hours of devotion and for your many words of encouragement

Lillian Bernard called one day and I guessed she detected the frustration in my voice as I was reading and refining the chapters of the book. She suggested that I ask different people to read a chapter each and offered to read the first chapter. She gave some scholarly edits that piqued my thoughts and made me conscientious as I navigated the other chapters for revision. Thanks Lillian.

Allison Levy Watson my newly acquired daughter also gave some input into to the earlier chapters. Energetic, resourceful and aspiring to be a great leader her input and questions steered me to include stories I probably would have overlooked. My gratitude for your support will be cherished for a life time.

Thanks to Ellis and my pastor, Rev. Cloyd for their dialogue about boxing. Their expert tips helped to renew and verify my facts as I toiled with aligning my career with the boxing phenomenon. Their enthusiasm about the sport furthered my idea of its connection to leadership. Thanks for the blessing.

Steve Brent and Jill Duero final editing helped to assure all commas, quotation marks and other elements were properly used. Thanks for your expertise.

My sister Louise who did not read any chapters pitched in and ran errands giving me uninterrupted time to write. Her willingness and genuine spirit to anticipate my needs and do task without me asking made me feel less imposing and I really appreciated those many times she stepped up to the plate. Lou thanks for the sisterhood.

Finally I thank all of my former employees, employers, peers and friends for providing the milieu where I exercised my creative skills, learned the new and applied the art of leadership that led to a joyous career.

Positively Blessed,
Mary Edna Holt Ashley

INTRODUCTION

WITHOUT A DOUBT, leadership for me was no crystal stairs. Yet I can confidently proclaim that the chaos, endless struggles, unanticipated disappointments, and numerous successes that satiated my soul and spirit empowered me to have a soulful experience. My career far exceeded my dreams. It resembled the hayride that I so desperately yearned for in my adolescent years.

I used to beg my mother to let me go to the beach, not just in a car—but in a truck on a hayride. Her answer was always no because she viewed it as risky and unsafe.

Yet when I saw all those kids on the back of that truck filled with hay and piled high, I dreamed of riding on that hay. I wanted to experience the ecstasy of the struggle to stay on top of the hay. They were rocking, bumping, jumping up, and falling down while trying to keep their bottoms on top. In the midst of what Momma perceived to be risky and scary, my friends were having a good time. Each time they fell off the hay pile, they got back up on and were able to ride it out and get to the beach.

The Harris County Hospital District (HCHD) afforded me a career much like that hayride. It was fun, challenging, and rewarding. I worked hard. I stayed on top, and I got to the "beach."

Mastering the hayride branded me with an indelible sense of joy, satisfaction, and pride during my passionate thirty-seven-year leadership career. I want to share the overflowing of my career that may be linked to those now in the leadership business and to the future generations. Subsequently, I retired while I still felt vibrant, energetic, and intellectually fit to write a book about my leadership journey.

The framework for describing my leadership journey is based upon my years of watching and fascination with the professional boxing phenomenon. A brutal sport, professional boxing, like a leadership career, can be an unrelenting battle. The business leader's fight arena, however, is a psychological one. As different as boxing and leadership may appear to be, both demand stamina, skills, and courage in order to be effective and to take as well as give the jabs, punches, uppercuts, and low blows as duly required.

Granted, leadership is no spectator sport nor is it for the faint at heart, but it is for those who develop the right knockout punch and who learn how to get up off the canvas and who become champions. Having had the opportunity to work as a nursing assistant, licensed vocational staff nurse, staff registered nurse, head nurse, supervisor, assistant director, director, chief nursing officer, and chief nursing executive, I can authentically share some experiences that may help transform careers.

When you love what you do, you don't mind the pain. Boxers engage inside a ring where they receive physical blows that may knock them down on to a canvas that catches them. Similarly, leaders are involved in psychological battles and may receive intellectual blows that may knock them down to their mental canvas. Both boxers and leaders have to get up off the canvas to be a winner.

My perceptions about boxing evolved during my formative years and continued in marriage. I listened to boxing matches over the radio with my dad when I was growing up, and I have been married for thirty-eight years to Ellis who watches sports on TV every day of the week no matter what. Boxing is a familiar scene on the televisions throughout my home, in my den, bedroom, and outside patio.

Whether I like it or not, I hear Ellis's moaning, groaning, and saying, "Get him, man. Get him, man," a million times. Sometimes I pause to watch boxing and listen to my husband's unsolicited verbal comments or his response to my inquiring mind. One of the things that I notice is no matter how beat-up the boxers are, they get up off the canvas and return for more. Never losing sight of the goal to win and achieve that round, the boxer gets upon his feet stumbling, eyes blackened and swollen, blood oozing from a cut, and starts punching and punching. He reestablishes his comeback power and keeps going; otherwise, the opponent steals his destiny.

The stamina, will, and courage to keep going in spite of the bruises and many rounds to go, even with the adversary right there in his face, gets the boxer right back up. That mind-set empowered me. My eyes secretly photographed this scenario, stored it in the darkroom of my brain, to be flashed periodically as a vivid reminder when I encountered mountains and molehills in my life and throughout my career. It was and is a fixed reminder that I too could take the crushing blows and get back up off the canvas.

I liken my progression in leadership at each level to that of boxers: featherweight, super featherweight, middleweight, super middleweight, light heavyweight, middle heavyweight, and super heavyweight champions. Each rank's criteria differentiate the division of achievement. The boxers' physical weight determines their rank, whereas the leaders' rank is determined by the weight of responsibility and accountability. Both leadership and boxing require superb skills to be a champion.

No matter how hard boxers are knocked down, they get up because they are all champions. There are boxers who had the speed, the knockout punch, and the courage, yet never earned the title of champion. Nonetheless, they were champions at heart because they gave their best and stayed on the course. Most often, only a rare few boxers are able to progress from one weight division to the other. There are several that have moved up within the same range, i.e., lightweight to welterweight to middleweight.

Oscar De la Hoya accomplished several ranks that included the super featherweight, lightweight, light welterweight, welterweight, light middleweight, and middleweight. Many boxers, such as Michael Spinks, Jeff Fenech, and Wilfred Benitez have achieved different ranks within the same division. Sugar Ray Leonard put on extra weight to fight in the light heavyweight division. However, to be his best he needed to stay in the middleweight division, his ideal position.

Most often, a boxer stays in his or her rank and attempts to be the best while never giving up on becoming a champion, with the ultimate goal of holding the title. Heavyweight champions Joe Louis, Muhammad Ali, and George Foreman only fought in the heavyweight division, where they excelled and earned the title. In Houston, I am among a rare few among leaders who traversed seven different ranks and moved to the highest position in nursing leadership within the same organization.

This book is for leaders who want to achieve, move higher up the ranks, or just stay where they are and be a champion. While it is not a recipe book, you will find stories and acts of courage that may help you face the challenges and opportunities inherent in leadership roles. You too can get up off that canvas!

CHAPTER 1

Mind over Matter

LEAVING BEHIND MY beloved career was more difficult than I anticipated because my physical, spiritual, and psychological self missed challenges and opportunities that catalyze me into action. As I toyed with the idea of retirement, the anticipated void in my life conjured up images that left me in agony—the requisite moving of the rocking chair, gardening, and making strawberry preserves. This is not what I like to do. This is not who I am. I read and studied Rick Warren's book, *Purpose Driven Life*, and said to myself, *Working, this is my purpose. Do I have another purpose? Um, I could write that book that I have often contemplated.*

Bemoaning my retirement, I engaged in a lot of prayer and meditation, and my Sunday school class had to listen as I battled with my conflicts. Finally, I submitted my three-month retirement notice.

First, I told Carla, my administrative assistant, my decision to retire. She began to cry and tried to get me to change my mind. Carla literally became ill and moped around for several weeks. She knew I had anticipated writing a book but did not realize I would retire to do it. I felt like I had betrayed Carla. Once I made David, my boss, aware of my intentions, and as the word got out, I was inundated by many surprised questions, well wishes, and sad expressions of my retiring. These emotional responses further escalated my anxieties about my decision, yet I forged forward.

Ellis, my husband and sports enthusiast, who retired ten years ago, remarked, "You might as well retire while you are at the top of your career rather than hang around like some star football and baseball players do. They soon become ineffective and start to decline in their ability to produce at the same level." The reality of his remarks was profound because I too, an avid sports fan, had observed this repeatedly happening to top players but had not applied it to my situation. These players' dreams were to be the best and retire at the top of their game, yet they were holding on to the past rather than embracing the future for other possibilities.

In essence, a purpose-driven life is a journey that has to be orchestrated in different directions in order to fully maximize a purpose as one enters the different phases of life. A new era of my life was upon me. As I mulled over Ellis's philosophical morsels, I reflected on the positives that a book has the potential for instilling lasting memories, even after I have departed this earthly life. This was soothing to my soul and spirit.

Sharing some of my book ideas with different people on the leadership framework, I received a litany of how to and what to write. I was amazed at the number of people who inquisitively or persnickety said, "Oh, I thought you were going to give us the lowdown on your hospitals," or "Oh boy, I want to read about the district because you ought to have some juicy stories to tell." Having worked in a public hospital system that is frequently in cross fire with the county commissioners and strapped for resources, some people seemed to think there were untold secrets to exploit. There are none.

Many of my peers, employees, and a few board members offered their perspective and expressed that my story would be significantly important to others as well as the hospital district. One particular comment was by Betty, "I want my daughter to read about a woman that I personally know and can vouch for her credibility in achieving success the old-fashioned way—hard work, tenacity, and perseverance, with integrity." This swelled my heart with pride, yet I felt humbled from such revelation.

Then there was my neighborhood friend Ina who said, "Mary, your ability to overcome setbacks, orchestrate your career, and sustain a joyful commitment to your organization has to be shared with others. Your journey is a great motivator for others and will be a constant reminder of how success evolves when you enjoy what you are doing, staying focused and purposeful." Ina constantly called me and encouraged me to get started and was always following up to be sure I was on track. Her interest in seeing me write created that urgency and thirst that I needed to get me going and sustain my drive.

Torn between my initial desire to write a theoretical book on leadership and the unsolicited advice that also made real good sense, I pondered, *What is the best approach, and what do I want leaders to remember?* A pivotal turn in my brainstorming and decision making came from advice received from an editor with the *Houston Chronicle* newspaper. I sat next to him at a nursing recognition program where I was the keynote speaker. As he was reading my bio, he suddenly turned to me and asked, "What made you retire so early?" I explained to him that my goal was to write a book on leadership using boxing as a frame of reference.

I gave him a brief overview of my intentions. He acknowledged that my theory sounded interesting and made sense, but he told me, "Write more about yourself. Folks are going to want to know how a young gal from La Marque, Texas, rose from a nursing assistant to become the chief nurse executive for the hospitals and clinics of the Harris County Hospital District. There are hundreds of books on leadership, but your personal journey will be more exciting to the people who know you and will appeal to others."

That approach amazed me as I momentarily thought, *Who, me?* My mind traveled to my yesteryears while growing up in La Marque, when no one was interested in me or what I was doing. I was awestruck. Here is someone, a stranger, telling me to write about my life. I immediately urged myself to forget about those years of rejections, times when my dignity was assaulted, and instead embrace the fruitful years of my life that have given me much satisfaction and joy. As I stood and walked toward the podium to deliver my address, I had to redirect my thoughts from the anticipated book to the speech at hand.

Immediately when the program was over, I got into my car and began to revisit my career dash from 1969 to 2006. Aligning my leadership experiences in a framework that aspiring and experienced leaders could glean some pointers for their personal leadership journey heightened my desire to share my story. I felt like the proverbial kid in the toy store. Poverty, prayer, and perseverance were my strongholds. My mind raced through the years, acknowledging the bumps, twists, and turns in the road, but more importantly, the joys and successes.

That day, I convinced myself that my story was not an egotistical rattling but a compelling journey of a young girl from a meager background armed with a rich spirit who got up "off the canvas" and carved out of her struggles a legacy. "Yes! I will write about myself, using parts of the boxer's metaphor as the frame of reference to depict my life and leadership career."

Leadership Point

Round One

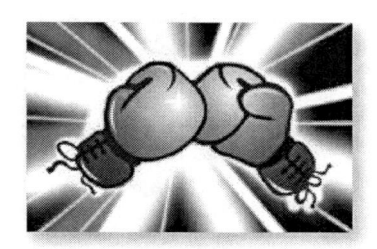

Develop a Knockout Punch

1. Identify and refine your strengths for maximum level of success.
2. Brand your leadership by your effective punches.
3. Understand that battles are won in the center of the ring.
4. Value your strengths.
5. Share your techniques with peers and subordinates.

CHAPTER 2

Unintentional Foundation for Leadership

MY LEADERSHIP JOURNEY started long before I recognized the elements that were shaping and have shaped my philosophy. Many things have influenced my growing and becoming. Notwithstanding my education and experiences, the upbringing and values instilled in me by my parents, Buster and Ella Mae, have a far-reaching impact. Neither parent had more than a second grade education, but they were stalwarts in framing my persona.

Whereas their contribution to my leadership adroitness was not intentionally designed, it laid the foundation for my life. Their teaching laid the bricks and the mortar that fortified integrity, tenacity, and perseverance—ideals that inadvertently constitute effective leadership. They taught me how to "get up off the canvas" when knocked down and not to spend a lot of time wallowing in self-pity. When I recall some of my parents' principles and ways of doing, a smile creeps across my face as I appreciate the thought of what they would do or say in certain situations.

Growing up in a large family where money was scarce, we lived in poverty in La Marque, Texas. It is a small city, located thirteen miles from Galveston and three miles from Texas City. People did not raise animals or grow gardens, and there was no housing designated for the poor. We lived in rented apartments and houses, some with outdoor toilets, until I finished school and was able to help my family buy their own home. The chemical plants in Texas City provided the main source of work. Men who were lucky to get a job there earned a nice income. My father was not one of them.

We were influenced by two strong-willed parents. I, the second oldest among my six siblings, was reared in a close-knit family where we looked out for each other. Love, respect, and good behavior were requirements in our house. My mother was guided by spiritual values that emphasized faith, thankfulness, and patience while my dad was guided by his ego of self-reliance. "If it is to be, it's up to me." He was proud, independent, and meticulous about us having a good, honorable reputation no matter what our circumstances.

Undaunted by the albatross of scant resources, low-paying jobs or no work to support a large family, my parents were not stymied. They were steadfast and unwavering in their beliefs. Momma constantly reminded us that we were blessed and to give thanks for what we had. We said our blessings before whatever we ate, whether a grand, luscious meal or one scrapped together from what was available in the kitchen. We prayed prayers that were consistent and filled with thanksgivings.

My dad had two sons who were older than my mom, and they were more like our uncles. Daddy's sister died at an early age, so he raised her five children along with his sons, and now he and my mother had seven more children. Experienced at handling a big family, his patience and ability to organize us kids into a manageable group within the walls of a three-room apartment was a skillful act.

Growing up in Brenham, Texas, he dug graves for a living and proudly boasted of the skillful manner in which he carried out each digging. A short muscular-built man, he masterfully described a work of art that he put his heart and soul into because he loved it.

Frequently, he explained how he carved out a grave:

> I took dat shovel, and with one hand I raised it up, stabbed it into da dirt. Den I took my foot and pushed da shovel while at the same time rotating it a bit to da right and to da left to get it deep 'nough into da ground so I could pick up an ample amount of dirt. I kept doing dis till da grave was dug. I was careful to lay da dirt in certain piles so dat when I covered da grave I used the right ones first. I turned out a smooth bed for whoever was in dat casket. Man, I tell ya. Ya could tell my graves from all of da others.

Daddy gained a new skill and passion when he moved to La Marque and became a mortar maker for construction jobs that paid union rates. He quickly garnered the skills and repeatedly shared with us: "I wuz da one who taught doze young whippasnappers how to make dat mortar, and dey had to do it right."

When he worked steadily for a few months, we lived a routine life. The first thing Daddy did when he got his paycheck was to come home with seven bags of Dentler's potato chips. We squealed with delight when we saw him coming down the street with a bag of groceries in each hand. We chanted, "Chips, chips, chips!" Those were the good times. Daddy was fiercely proud of that job and being a union member. Thus, he only worked jobs that paid union wages.

The drawback was that the union frequently engaged in strikes, and when the weather was rainy or unaccommodating, especially in the wintertime, Daddy could not work. Many months of each year we were at rock bottom. We did not even qualify for governmental support because we had two parents. On the other hand, my daddy would never have accepted it because he was too proud to take handouts or to "beg" as he often called it.

During the time Daddy was out of work and there was not enough food, the lights, water, and gas were frequently disconnected. When we got a pink slip in the mail from one of the utility companies indicating the service would be discontinued, we would hurry home from school and watch the clock because we knew if five o'clock came and the utility had not been disconnected, we would have another night to use it. The toughest times were when school started and there were no new clothes or shoes. A sad feeling shaded the excitement of the first day of school, but when we had new or different clothes, we were happy to go.

On occasions when our clothes were different but not new, it was because the people Mom worked for gave us clothes that Momma altered to fit us. When we saw Momma coming down the street with a large cloth sack on her back, tantamount to seeing one's mother toting a shopping bag, we ran to meet her. We anxiously awaited a peek into the sack to see who would be the lucky one. Momma would say, "It is not enough for everybody, but I know who got something the last time. After you all try them on, I will decide who gets what based on how it looks on you or how much work I have to put into it to make it fit." Since there were four girls, we held our breath for the decision.

Regularly there were Christmases without a tree, toys, or a turkey. No self-pity was allowed. I recall Daddy getting up on those mornings with a happy smile on his face saying, "Y'all better hurry up and get up so ya can play with yer toys." He then went to each bed, pulling off the covers and tickling us until we were in a good mood. Throughout the day, he made reference to the imaginary turkey, using expressions such as, "I hope ya Momma don't burn dat turkey," or "Oh, boy, don't dat turkey smell good?"

We laughed and said, "Daddy, we ain't got no turkey." He replied, "Yeah, you do. Just sniff ya nose." And then he would sniff and sniff again and declare how great the smell was until we would all chimed in, "The turkey smells good." Laughter could be heard throughout the house. Even though it was not a traditional Christmas spread, whatever Momma was cooking, it was going to be good. She was an excellent cook.

At some point, Daddy would say, "Come on y'all. Let me tell you a story." We jumped up and down clapping our hands. We were in for a treat. My father was known for his storytelling and "hurrahing" (saying something humorous about a situation). In spite of our circumstances, we enjoyed happy and fun times as he kept us laughing at all kinds of stories. Many of them were not true, but the way he dramatized them kept us motionless and glued to every word that was spoken. We hung on to the stories. As he poked fun and used humor in the situation, feelings of disappointment were diverted to more pleasant thoughts, and we soon were laughing and having fun. Sometimes other kids from the neighborhood joined us and enjoyed his sense of humor too.

They would ask, "Mr. Buster, can we come in?"

Dad always said, "Sho ya can as long as ya pay 'tention." "I will, I will," each of them eagerly yelled out.

Most of them did not have a daddy living with them, so my dad took time to talk with them, giving fatherly attention and advice.

Off and on we had a television because we bought one during Daddy's steady working period, but when he was out of work, the missed payments resulted in it being repossessed. Daddy emphasized that even though the television was gone, we could still learn from the radio. His theory was, if you can sit and listen, you can learn and be smart. Many times all of the kids would huddle together on a pallet and listen to programs, boxing matches, and baseball games.

We had to sit still and be quiet in order to hear and not disrupt others. Later, not necessarily the same day, there were questions in the form of a game. If Daddy had only two pieces of his favorite Juicy Fruit gum but all of us wanted it, he would make us compete for it. He asked questions about the program or the game we had listened to. His favorite quip was, "You shoulda been listening. That's why you carry dat thang on ya shoulders." He handed the gum to the person who got the answer right.

Daddy was adamant that all of us learn to play dominoes so we could learn how to count "in our head," for he would not let us use our fingers to count. He believed that if you could add quickly you would always know what your grocery bill was going to be before you got to the checkout counter. He prided himself when purchasing groceries he approached the checkout counter with a basket of groceries and announced what the total bill was, without the taxes. Once the clerk confirmed, he turned to the one who had gone to the store with him, and while pointing to his head, he says with a smile, "I don't need no cash register, pencil, nor paper to add up my groceries 'cause I can add in my head."

Dad taught us how to work competitively, independently, and have fun. One of his favorite ways was to get us involved in shelling pecans, and we loved it. Neighbors who went to the country usually shared large bags of pecans with us. To get them shelled, Dad had us play what he called the pecan game, and he set the rules. The game began with us sitting on the floor in a circle. He gave each of us ten pecans to shell. The object of the game was to produce each half of the pecan in a whole piece. The person who had the largest number of whole pieces was the winner and got to eat some of the crumbled pieces.

We had no pecan crushers, hammers, or devices to help crack the pecan. We used whatever we had, such as shoes, teeth, and our strength. Each person worked independently; age, size, or gender did not matter. You had to finish all ten pecans, or you could pull out at any time, but you could not play the next game.

We were engaged; we laughed, joked, and competed against one another. There was a lot of struggling during a game. It was difficult to get a whole piece of pecan out until you got the hang of it. Sometimes, just as you were easing the pecan out of the shell, it would crumble into small pieces that could bring you to heartbreaking tears. You did not have time to fret before Daddy said, "Don't worry 'bout dat ole pecan. Get anotta one and keep going." When the game was over, he inspected and counted the pecans.

At each stack he found something positive to say using a humorous quip such as, "Boy, ya keep on working like dis, I'm go hang out ya shingles as the champion of pecan pickers." His way of encouraging and motivating us kept us going. When the next game started, he issued ten more pecans to shell. Usually we played two or three games, and if other children were present, they were allowed to participate. The pecan game resulted in Mom having a ready supply of pecans to make desserts and salads.

Reflecting on the games, my lessons learned were the following: Do your best. Use what you got. Be competitive and creative. Quality and quantity count. Earn rewards for doing the best, and try it again. Whatever you start, finish it. Neither Dad nor I realized at that time that these games were principles for working and leading others.

Our biggest and most frequent family outing was going fishing all day long any Saturday we could on the Texas City dike or to the Hitchcock fishing hole. Both Momma and Daddy passionately loved fishing, whereas we submitted to the eight-hour torture because we had no choice. Momma always looked for twigs, driftwood, and rocks to take home where she turned them into beautiful doodads and whatnots to sit on the shelves and windowsills. She was very artistic but never had the opportunity to cultivate her skill through training or education; however, she enjoyed the long, meticulous hours she put into each one of her crafts.

When we arrived home from fishing, the older kids cleaned the fish no matter if they were six inches or two feet long; most of them were six inches. Momma cooked them, then sat down, and picked the bones out of the fish to ensure they did not get caught in our throat. After she had completed seven piles of fish, we were allowed to eat. As we grew older, that job was delegated downward until each child was mature enough to pick the bones. On our lucky days, neighbors gave us a big garfish, which did not have small bones, and Momma let us eat without her prepicking the bones.

Because there were many siblings, we had to share everything among each other and other kids if they were there. Frequently, kids hung around our house as we were growing up. Kenneth was there all the time, so we thought of him as a brother. He treated Mom and Dad well and usually bought Dad a package of Chesterfield cigarettes, which he loved. Kenneth was an only child, so he enjoyed the loud, loving family atmosphere we had at our little house. He had an allowance, and he brought goodies and shared them with us, and he ate whatever Mom fixed. Sometimes he joked about what it was, but Momma would say to him, "Don't ask any questions. Just eat. It will fill your belly up." He would laugh and fall down on the floor. Daddy would say to him, "Boy, ya legs too long for ya to fall out like dat." We all joined in the laughter.

Momma instilled in us to go to church and work in the church. We belonged to a small church where our family constituted half of its membership. Rev. Hardeman, our preacher and pastor, was a little man with a powerful voice who taught us the Bible. He had strabismus, a condition where the eye wanders, and thus when he shouted out orders for us to do something, everybody moved because we could not tell which one of us he was actually looking at. We loved and respected him.

All seven kids went to church all day on Sundays and worked on Saturdays to clean the church or help sell dinners to the community to raise funds for the church. In the summertime, there was the two-week vacation Bible school, which we loved. It was the only vacation we knew about.

Momma, a leader in the church, made sure we took an active role, and she sacrificially paid her $1.25 dues each week, even when it meant the family was going without. Her faith was strong. We recited speeches at each special occasion until we reached the age of fourteen. Then we had to help coordinate the program. None of us wanted to do speeches because we were nervous and dreaded getting on stage. Admittedly, I enjoyed seeing the people in the audience say "Amen," and "Amen, that was good."

By the time I was fourteen, I was the young adult program coordinator and considered that a highly responsible role and eagerly served in it until I started college. As a matter of fact, each of my sisters, Barbara, Louise, and Ella, and I have been committed leaders in our churches throughout our adult lives, serving in multiple roles. Momma continued her work in the church until her death, and it appears that my sisters and I are headed in the same direction.

Growing up, I had to stay in the house a lot due to frequent asthmatic episodes. I did not want my family to see how I was suffering, which always alarmed them when the attacks progressed to a state where I had to go to the emergency room. The only way I got to see the doctor was on an emergency basis. We had no insurance, money, or transportation. I saw the pain in my parents' eyes when I began wheezing. Mom said, "Oh my God, that old asthma is bothering you again." We waited and prayed to see how things would turn out.

Mom rubbed Vicks salve on my chest and made me drink a cup of warm water or used whatever home remedy someone had shared with her. Occasionally, she asked Mr. Lane, our neighbor, also an asthmatic, for some of his medicine, which he gave to me, and I got better quickly. Other times my asthma had to wear off, or it progressed to an emergency state.

I felt guilty that I caused them to worry and had fleeting tinges of jealousy toward my siblings because of their freedom from asthma. In an attempt to prevent the asthma attacks, sometimes I deliberately stayed inside and refrained from running around outside, playing jump rope or softball, which I thought brought on the asthma.

When staying inside alone was my prevention strategy, to pass the time I created a different look for one of the rooms in the house. Our home, less than modest, was clean and orderly. Torn paper lined the walls; bare floors with cracks permitted a flow of air and a view under the house.

Most would think little could be done to enhance its appearance, but I reached way down into my creative spirit and came up with ideas. I made curtains and chair covers out of old clothes, changed the rickety furniture around, or did something that was noticeably pleasing. Improvising and struggling to make a change challenged and excited me. Years later I learned in nursing school the scientific term for it was "adrenalin rush." Nonetheless, I could not wait to see the finished product. I wanted to surprise everybody when they came inside.

Other times, I daydreamed of my life as a nurse. I imagined how I looked in the white shoes, uniform, and the cap with the black stripe. I envisioned the patients I would help, and as my dreams became bigger, I thought about the money I would make to help my family. My inner thoughts took me to the place I wanted to be in life. Wow! This dream was powerful and so real to me. At that instance, I enjoyed being in the house by myself, so I really let my mind run wild without interference from my siblings. I did not want them to know what I was dreaming. This was my secret key to the future.

When classmates talked about going to college, I didn't mumble a word to them, fearing they would say, "How in the world are you going to college? You all are too poor. You are not going." I didn't dare mention my aspirations to my parents because I did not want them burdened with knowing I wanted to go to Prairie View A&M University when they could not afford to send me. They often expressed that each of us was going to be educated, which to them meant all their kids finished high school. Their goal was for us to get a good job. I dreamed bigger and continued to do what I had been taught and believed: "If you pray for something, it will happen."

I began praying about going to college and becoming a nurse in the ninth grade, partly inspired by my friend Billie Lou who bragged no end about her sister Ruby Jean's white uniform, cap, and shoes. Thus, when I saw her I was mesmerized by the beauty of that uniform. Secondly, I felt a little smug about what I wanted to be because most of the other girls in my class talked about becoming teachers or secretaries.

The third contributor was my many trips to the emergency room for severe asthma attacks. The compassion I experienced from the nurses made me feel better, so I wanted to help people do the same. Enthralled on becoming a nurse, I dreamed of it all the time. Perhaps I understood early in life, "If the mind can conceive it, then I can achieve it." I believed the money for college would literally be on the kitchen table.

Graduation night, I wandered almost in a tiptoe fashion into the kitchen, peering out of the corners of my eyes as I looked expectedly on the table for the money. Quickly raising the tablecloth up, I looked under the table to see if the money had fallen to the floor. It was not there. I did not want to sabotage my dream, my prayer, by thinking negatively, so I consoled myself, *I got time. College doesn't start till September.*

My strong faith sustained my hope that the money would show up in a few days. Not sharing this with anyone, I kept looking for several weeks. Each night I went to bed in anticipation that my prayers would be answered in the morning. Months passed, the money did not appear on the table. I didn't know what happened, but as Momma had taught, I didn't question God. I soon got a job working at Mae's Diner in Texas City as a dishwasher. Unfortunately, it lasted about three hours.

As I began to work, the lady told me to keep the spoons stacked when I wasn't washing dishes. Each time I stacked them, they fell over on to the floor. That happened two times, and each time she rolled her eyes at me in disgust. I did not know how to keep them from falling and was too scared to ask. The third time it happened, she said, "You are fired, and get out of here right now." Shocked and scared, I stood there bewildered, wondering what to do.

I ran to the phone and called a cab although I did not have any money to pay for it. Mr. Conley, owner of the local taxicab company, came to pick me up. Boohooing and jabbering, I barely explained myself as he kept asking what was wrong. Finally, I quieted down. I blubbered, "I got fired because I could not stack the spoons to keep them from falling."

He smiled knowingly. "You probably should have stacked them into two or three piles instead of one, but don't worry, come work for me at the cab stand as a dispatcher."

When I reached home, eyes dried and feeling defeated, I told Momma what happened and that I needed money to pay for the cab. She went to the door, but Mr. Conley had gone. I told her that he said I could work for him. I thought to myself, *I hope he meant it.* I waited a couple of hours and called him to ask if he was going to let me work. "Of course," he reassured. "Yes, I meant that."

That was a blessing because in the early sixties, in small towns, there were no jobs for black females other than domestic work or dishwashers. I did a lot of that kind of work because I helped Momma clean houses, and I cleaned, ironed, and babysat for one of our neighbors, Mrs. Hightower. I also earned an independent domestic worker status, so I worked by myself on some jobs. I didn't like the title "maid" or having to ride in the backseat of the car when my boss picked me up or brought me home. Nevertheless, I always did good work and did my best because excellent results made me proud.

I imagined that the houses I cleaned were my own and thus I was able to create for a moment the right ambiance for me to enjoy what I was doing. Momma taught me that no matter what kind of work you do, as long as it is honest and aboveboard, be proud and do whatever it takes to do your best. From my domestic work I gained creative skills that helped me to become good at decorating my own house. I embraced Momma's work ethics and was well grounded in the art of hard work.

Being poor, frequently rejected and disrespected in the outside world motivated me to compensate by being dependable, creative, and hardworking. If my life destiny was to change, getting knocked down and wallowing on the canvas would not help. I had to get on up and keep moving in the right direction. I always held myself to a "you can do this" standard.

My entry into the real work world was the dispatcher job at the cab stand. I was proud of that job. My boss for domestic work had intentionally ignored me all day, except when she was forced to talk to me in order to give me extra work to do. On the contrary, my new boss, Mr. Conley, was a true gentleman and distinguished how a supervisor or boss should treat their subordinates. He often complimented, "Holt, you are such a good worker, so dependable, and I am glad you work for me." Those commendations empowered me to give 100 percent willingly, and I derived immense satisfaction. Long before becoming a leader, I recognized the power of saying thank you as a motivator.

For the first time ever, I was respected and appreciated. Someone other than my parents or church members at last gave me a compliment and let me participate. I had so longed for that because I finished high school without ever having a teacher show any interest in me or include me in certain functions that indicated equal respect or care. Such assignments as erasing the blackboard, helping to grade papers, taking names of students who were disruptive during the teacher's absence, or running simple errands were given only to those students whom the teacher favored.

Usually they favored the light-skinned students or those whose parents had important jobs such as teachers, preachers, business owners, or equivalent status symbol. I, among several other students, was never chosen because we were the have-nots. Some of the kids ridiculed me about my short nappy hair and well-worn clothes and said such things as, "Those Holts are so poor and raggedy."

I was taught to stand tall and did not let the ridicule faze or demean me. Instead, I focused on the educational opportunities that the classroom provided me. Not always having the resources to support the essentials was often an inconvenience, but I persevered as best I could. I recall not having two cents to buy white milk or three cents to buy chocolate milk for break time. The teacher went from desk to desk to collect money from each student to order milk. When she reached my desk, I said with a straight face "I don't want any"—too ashamed to say I didn't have the money. I think she knew.

When other students were drinking theirs, sometimes a student would say, "How come you don't have no milk"? I retorted, "I don't like it." My posture of cool indifference got them off my back, and there was no further discussion.

Lunchtime also presented its share of strain. In elementary school the teacher made us tear open our bags, say grace, and share. We got to choose who we wanted to share with. Most of the kids had nicely wrapped sandwiches or a fried chicken leg, whereas my lunch on many occasions consisted of a tiny bit of tuna thinly spread on two pieces of bread wrapped in bread paper or brown paper bag paper. That made me not want to share, and often no one picked me. It's hard to say which situation embarrassed me more, having no lunch or having scantily spread tuna sandwiches.

I recall the time Mom made our lunch with a baked sweet potato. I was so anxious about lunchtime that day, so as soon as I got to school I threw my lunch into another girl's locker who was eating in the cafeteria. At the end of the day as the teacher checked the lockers, she found it and asked, "Whose baked potato is this?" I sat there trembling while wanting to confess but could not do it. She threw the potato out after no one claimed it. The kids laughed and talked about someone bringing a sweet potato for lunch for the next few days.

Times when I did not have any paper to write on, I did not always ask someone for a sheet because I borrowed so frequently. I just wrote on the back of a used sheet and turned in the assignment, knowing this behavior would bring a reprimand from the teacher. But I'd rather do that than have the student say, "You don't ever have any paper." Humiliation from my peers was more painful than a teacher's reprimand.

In the second grade, we were practicing our writing, where you repeat one letter of the alphabet continuously on each line of a sheet of paper. We were doing the *H* in capital letters and upon completion printed our names on the back of the paper and turned it in. After all the papers were collected, the teacher started going through the papers. When she got to a certain paper, she smiled and exclaimed, "What beautiful handwriting this is! Who wrote this? Who wrote this?" She turned the paper over to see whose writing it was, but when she saw my name she just frowned and huffed, "Oh, this is Holt's paper!" She put the paper down and did not speak another complimentary word about it and went on to gush about other students' papers.

Crushed by the teacher's insensitivity, Daddy's instructions rang in my ear, "Don't let nobody make you cry. Holts don't cry." Bravely, I got up off the canvas and sat there stiff and unfazed, amid my classmates' snickers. I did not shed a tear. Even though I had a nice penmanship, from then on I often denied and suppressed that skill by writing messy. I could not bear to place myself in jeopardy of getting noticed, only to be rejected in the process.

Later, in the ninth grade, I was with a group of students riding in a car driven by a teacher, on our way to the New Homemakers of America Society (NHA) meeting in Silsbee, Texas. We had to wear navy blue skirts and white blouses. I did not have a navy blue skirt nor could Momma afford to buy one. On top of that, she did not have anything to make for my lunch and had tried to talk me out of going.

I begged, "I won't be hungry, and I can wait until I get home to eat."

Momma got creative and looked for a skirt lying around that she could dye. Under the mattress where we kept clothes, she found one but stopped dead in her tracks and declared, "Oh shoots, I don't have a dime to buy that dye."

"Momma, Momma! I know what I can do!"

Momma lifted her eyebrows. "What? What will you do?" I then volunteered my brother Walter and I to go out hunting for soda water bottles and then sell them, like we often did to scrape up some money. She shook her head, smiling. "Okay, go ahead. But don't y'all go too far."

Walter and I got his old homemade wagon, and we trotted out of the house looking in ditches and trash for glass bottles. After a couple of hours, we had a wagon full of bottles to be redeemed at two cents per bottle. We sold them, split the profit. I had enough to buy the dye, and Walter gave me a nickel to buy something for lunch on the trip.

Mom did her best dying the skirt, but it had a lot of streaks in it. Because I desperately wanted to go on that trip, I wore the thing anyway. While we were on our way, the group and I were laughing and having a good time when the teacher looked in the rearview mirror and chided, "Holt, what in the world are you laughing so hard about with that ole streaked-up skirt that you have on?" My friend Billie Lou blurted out, "Ain't nothing wrong with her skirt." Though the teacher did not respond, I was still thoroughly humiliated. I had tried so hard to draw attention away from that skirt and left home hoping no one would pay much attention to it. After that little dustup, I wanted to withdraw from the NHA, but stuck it out.

Getting the dispatcher job was a new beginning for me, a lifesaver—financially, emotionally, and sociologically. The men whom I dispatched calls to were polite and respectful. I loved answering the phone and talking to the customers, making many friends without ever meeting them face to face. Since I interacted with them on a frequent basis, I was able to anticipate where they were going and attempted to get them there on time.

Frankly, I enjoyed knowing that someone valued me and what I contributed. It brought out the best in me. Only making $20 per week, I saved $15. When I had $50, I opened my first savings account and received a blue book that recorded my deposits. It was the first time a Holt had opened a bank account. That was a major accomplishment, and my parents were proud. Mom asked me to send Barb, my oldest sister, something once a month because she was in beauty school in Houston. Momma promised me that when Barb finished her training she would help me go to college. Out of the five dollars that I kept out for myself I saved a dollar a week so that each month I could send Barb $5.

For one year, I dutifully saved each week for college. As I reviewed that little blue book weekly, it indicated that my seed was growing and so was my confidence. Often the family needed the money, but Momma firmly supported that it was for my college, and we would do without. When it was time to go to college I was thrilled I had saved enough to stay on campus at Texas Southern University in Houston for one entire semester. Mr. Conley took me to the bus station, and when I got out of the cab, he gave me some words of encouragement and $5. I was humbled to near tears.

When I arrived in Houston, Naomi, a girl I grew up with, met me at the bus station and showed me around the campus. It was scary to be away from home, and the fact that I had to sleep in a bed by myself was even more eerie. I was accustomed to sleeping with my three sisters. To have a bed all to myself, no sharing required, was a little intimidating at first; however I soon adapted and began to enjoy the roomy expanse.

I developed a strong sisterly friendship with Barbara, from Texas City. I rode home with her on the weekends. She always had lots of food from home and shared it with me. I felt awkward always taking and not having something to offer. She was a loving and caring person and told me not to worry that my family could not afford to send me packages. She had plenty for the both of us. I learned to play the card game bid whist, and Barbara and I were the team everyone wanted to beat. We studied but always had time on the weekend for those marathon card games. They were a lot of fun.

My money ran out after just one semester. Barb finished beauty school, moved to Pampa, Texas, and did not help me with tuition as promised. I found myself back at home, uncertain about what I was going to do but steadfast with desire and determination to continue chasing my dream to become a nurse.

Lack of available jobs forced me to return to domestic work, and I also peeled potatoes part-time at the Terrance Drive-in restaurant in Texas City. It was honest money, and it beat sitting around moaning and groaning about what I didn't have. The city bus route ended at the main street, so I had to walk almost a mile to the restaurant. Once I got there I had to enter through the back door to work for eight hours standing on my feet. I took pride ensuring the potatoes were peeled, sliced, and washed to perfection. I occasionally challenged myself to peel extra potatoes; even though it went unrecognized, my self-satisfaction barometer moved up another degree.

I worked as a domestic for a family and developed a friendship with their teenage son Dan. A first for me—a mutual relationship outside of my own culture. Dan was friendly and often followed me from room to room, sharing opinions on different subjects. It helped me to make friends when I integrated Alvin Junior College's Nursing Program. It puzzled me that Dan's mom and her friends did not find me worthy of conversation as I stood in the same room ironing for hours while they sat on the couch, gabbed, and ate. They never offered me a morsel of food. My stomach growled in vain as the only thing I had consumed all day was water.

Within a year, I applied to go to a nursing assistant school at John Sealy Hospital, which is now the University of Texas Medical Branch. The head of the nursing assistant program, a large woman with bouffant blond hair, chubby face, and red cheeks, was very positive and emphasized the importance of the work I would be doing. I was eager to get started. It was not difficult to absorb the information, and she was a master teacher. I rode the bus to Galveston each day while I completed the two-week course. This small achievement was a joyously tearful validation to me that success was not unreachable.

Upon graduation I was permitted to wear a white uniform with a royal blue collar, which distinguished it from the white uniform that I wore as a maid. That was a symbol of moving up, and now when neighbors and friends saw me, they would know I was making progress toward becoming a nurse.

I was hired to work the graveyard shift, 11:00 p.m. to 7:00 a.m. Because I had to catch the bus and the last one on the weekends arrived in Galveston at 6:00 p.m., I got to the hospital at 6:30 p.m. and sat in the lobby until 10:45 p.m. to start my shift. I marveled at working with sick people despite the fact that the job scope of the nurse's aide was limited. We bathed and fed patients; sterilized the aluminum bedpans, urinals, and water pitchers; and made beds. Nurse's aides were not allowed in the nurses' station.

Working in a seventy-seven-bed ward, I enjoyed walking up and down the aisles and ensuring that each of my patients had a shiny water pitcher and each pillow was fluffed, with the pillowcase opening turned to the left side. My knees buckled when patients called me Miss Holt because I thought that handle was for older persons or for white people only. My name, Miss M. Holt, NA, (nursing assistant), printed on my badge gave me respect, and I felt dignified. There was pride in knowing I could follow orders, make decisions, and help patients.

When I provided something as simple as helping patients get in and out of bed, most of them said, "I sure appreciate that." The power of thank you is addictive to my soul and spirit.

Being a self-starter and eager to learn tasks that were not in my job description, I was delighted when the licensed vocational nurses (LVN) I worked with taught me how to take vital signs. Wow! When I heard the heart beating through the stethoscope, I experienced an epiphany. I could not wait until my tour of duty so I could put that stethoscope around my neck to listen to heartbeats. It reaffirmed me that I desired to do more for the patients.

I loved this nursing assistant job, but my dreams to be an RN were stronger than ever. I struggled with how long it was going to take me to save enough money to go to Prairie View when I was only making forty cents an hour. Nonetheless, diligently each month I placed half of my pay into the savings account.

Seven months into the workforce as a nurse's aide, an announcement circulated that the hospital's one-year LVN program was accepting applicants based on their work performance, substantiated by a reference letter from their immediate supervisor. I applied, and my supervisor gave me a generous letter of support. I was accepted and worked sixteen hours on Saturdays and Sundays and one night during the week as a nursing assistant to support my schooling and help my family.

I did well in school and amassed a lot of friends, in particular, Rosie who was from La Marque. She agreed to let me ride with her, and I paid her on a weekly basis. That was really helpful as I assimilated into a new world of living and learning.

What really amazed me with my nursing studies was discovering and learning how the human body worked. I began to understand and see my asthma from a different perspective. It was really bothering me, so I sought help from the clinic at the hospital and got on a medical regime.

A friendly atmosphere of students and teachers made it an exciting time. The program director, Ms. Bender, and the teachers respected me and my work. Sometimes, all it takes for one to believe in oneself is for someone to believe in them. I loved studying and going to school. John, Rosie, Jessie Mae, and I studied together. It felt good to be competitive with my classmates in a friendly way. At home, my sisters, brothers, and niece helped me study by calling out questions for me. They too learned some medical terms and were proud to see me going to school. My clinical experience as a nursing assistant helped me to adapt quickly to the new procedures that LVNs performed.

Three weeks before graduation, I was hospitalized for two weeks with severe asthma that resulted in excessive absence from the clinical area. Upon returning to class, Ms. Bender informed me that I had been dropped from the nursing program because I did not have enough clinical hours to graduate. Shocked with disbelief, I almost keeled over; I felt weak so I took a seat. Ms. Bender saw that I was distraught but said, "There is nothing I can do."

I got up out of the chair and stood firmly before her and blurted out in a slow and deliberate tone, "Please, you have to do something."

She paused for a moment, then replied, "I will check with the accrediting agency to see if you can make up the time and go to the next state boards examination.

"Oh, thank you, thank you!"

"Don't get your hopes up too high, but I will do what I can."

I left her office and prayed all the way home, then literally sat by the phone until she called.

During the time I was waiting, Momma kept saying, "God will do what needs to be done."

Daddy said, "What you need to do is come out here on the porch and drink you some good old Nehi orange soda pop, and I am going to tell you about something that happened to me."

Just as he got my attention and was deep into the story, the phone rang. I jumped up, nervously ran to the phone, and screamed, "Hello, Ms. Bender, what did they say? What did they say?"

Ms. Bender softly replied, "Yes, you can make up your clinical days and go to state boards in July. Come into my office on Monday and fill out your papers."

I was overjoyed and thankful that my career was still on track. My classmates went to state boards in February while I stayed behind and made up clinical time. I did not feel disappointed; I was so glad I could make up my time. Five months later I took state boards and passed with flying colors. Inch by inch my dream was unfolding before me.

I began work as an LVN on the floor where I had worked as a nursing assistant. When I walked on to the floor with that white cap with the green stripe on it, a stethoscope around my neck, and that beautiful white uniform, it was a transforming experience. I had ambivalent feelings about feeling proud while trying to act as if it was just a routine day. A few of my friends still working there welcomed and congratulated me.

Patients and their families respected that cap and so did the visitors. We were taught in school that the cap was your dignity, and I believed and felt it. Looking in the mirror and seeing that cap on my head was affirmation that dreams do come true when you persevere.

It was even more exciting when someone that I knew from the community came to the hospital and saw me working as a nurse and would express, "I did not know you were a nurse. That's great." Occasionally, a former schoolmate saw me at work and offered well wishes.

I worked a lot of overtime to buy my mom some much-needed furniture and to save money to buy a car. When that day arrived, I got my friend Ora

Lee to take me to Houston to buy a Ford Mustang liked the one she owned. I prayed that I would be able to get it. They checked my credit and saw that I had excellent ratings with Zale's Jewelry and the Lerner Shops and had money for a down payment. When they approved me, it was like receiving a big, loud *yes* for my life and for everything I wanted to accomplish.

I got a yellow Mustang, four cylinders, standard shift, and no air-conditioning; but Marvin Gaye's song summed it best. It was my "pride and joy." My brothers teased me that it did not have enough horsepower, but I did not care. I had independent transportation but was always willing to share with my siblings. Louise and Walter drove it as much as I did. Occasionally, Dad would get up early in the morning and take a spin. He thought I did not know it, so I did not mention it.

Less than a year after practicing as an LVN and saving money to go to Prairie View, Alvin Junior College opened an associate degree nursing program in Alvin. My long-awaited opportunity to become an RN was a stone's throw away. Alvin was twelve miles from La Marque; thus, I could work as an LVN and go to school. I was eager to apply.

The director of the nursing program told me face to face: "I will allow you to enroll in the program only because I have to admit 'nigras' in order to receive grants and financial support from the government. You are not going to make it, so you should be content with being an LVN."

I looked her squarely in the face and said, "Just give me a chance. This is the career I dreamed of, and Alvin is my only opportunity."

Reluctantly, I was accepted into the second class.

It was at Alvin where I faced some of the toughest challenges in my life. Integration into this school was a new experience; however, I never imagined it would be as painful as I was about to discover. I lived in a segregated community, graduated from a segregated school, and had little experience in intermingling with another culture other than through domestic work.

It was eye awakening. The director levied harsh remarks against the black race. The class started with about ten to twelve blacks, but after the capping ceremony took place, numbers dwindled down to three—Sarah, Brenda, and me. We became good friends and had to lean on each other. I loved studying and trying to prove myself as a good student. Our clinical rotations took place at County Memorial Hospital in La Marque, my hometown. Some of my patients were people I knew; thus it was a privilege to care for them and share that I was studying to be an RN.

No matter the harsh treatment and disrespect, we stayed the course. Following my passion helped me to stay dedicated. It was difficult for me to understand the humiliation. Was the director really against us, or was she living out her personal beliefs? I relayed the stories of how I was treated to my family who urged me to quit. Blow by blow I stood up to the challenge. There were no knockouts, but there were many knockdowns. The way you respond to the opposition determines whether you get defeated or you win.

The nursing instructors did not treat us badly, meaning they never said harsh or demeaning remarks to us. Some ignored us or graded our papers with a fine-tooth comb. Sarah, Brenda, and I were separated during test taking—one to the front in the corner, one in the middle, and one in the back in the corner.

One teacher, Mrs. Matesen, broke the mold and became our friend; thus, we visited her at home and confided in her. The majority of the students treated us nicely. The class was a multigenerational, multiethnic group that expanded my sociological sphere of relationships.

To my surprise, one of the students was one of the women who sat in the living room of the home where I had worked as a maid. She wanted to know where she had met me before. I reminded her that I worked for a neighbor. Immediately her facial expressions changed to a frown, and I did not encounter her up close again.

Mrs. Wylie, the literature teacher, witnessed some of the treatment we received and asked why I didn't go somewhere else. I told her that my financial situation forced me to work; thus Alvin was my only opportunity to go to nursing school. She agreed and pointed out, "Mary, if you can endure this, it will make you strong for the work world, and you won't remember how bad it hurts."

She introduced me to the theater, giving me my first ticket to the Houston Music Theater to see the *Sound of Music*. This was a new experience for me. I got to the theater and enjoyed an evening of majesty. Subsequently, I bought season tickets, and to her credit, I have been an avid goer since.

One particular day, the director called us into her office and insulted us to no end, reminding us, like babies, to bathe each night and take off that underwear, wash them out so they would be fresh each day. On occasion, she impulsively entered into the nursing classroom and would scream, "Mary Edna, Sarah, and Brenda, get into my office this very minute. She would then issue threats and warnings. Weakened by the psychological blows, I stumbled out of the office, pumped myself up to a functional state, returned to class, and focused on the lecture.

Often she told me I would never make it because of asthma. At times I questioned that myself because I spent a lot of nights in the emergency room and barely got out in time to get to class. I just prayed she would not find out or that I would not have to miss a day of school. Thank God this did not happen.

Some days I was so short of breath I had to walk slowly to and from class, and my classmates would ask, "Are sure you can make it?" My answer was always, "I will be all right." Plagued by a long-standing history of respiratory embarrassment (as lung ailments were referred to in those days), there was no way I could hide it.

Shoulders hunched, prominent neck veins, loud musical wheezing were vivid clues as I gasped for breath. I was accustomed to getting either compassionate or crude remarks. When I used my glass DeVilbiss inhaler, it drew a lot of stares and questions, but when my body was desperate for oxygen all else became secondary.

My inhaler was noticeably large, so I only used it in public when I could not go any farther. I had to stop, lean against the wall, car, or the nearest resting place, and take a puff from the inhaler. Sara protected and shielded me as much as she could. Once I got some relief from my physiological embarrassment and began to breathe better, my personal and emotional embarrassment proceeded.

Marsha, a classmate whom I sat next to in one of the classes, gave me an extraordinary gift. I shared with her about my all-night emergency room experiences and how slow the ambulance was in getting there. She told me her husband worked for the Crowder Funeral Home. She would get him to take me to the emergency room. All I had to do was call him. Sure enough, when I required an ambulance again, I called, and he transported me a couple of times without charge during the two years we were in the nursing program.

Each time a Crowder ambulance arrived at my home, neighbors were inquisitive as to why an ambulance from the white funeral home was transporting me. I did not elaborate, but my mother reminded me that was God working behind the scene.

The nursing director told me not to watch the Reverend Martin Luther King's marches and sit-down strikes as she made crude remarks about his work. She also reminded Sarah and me that just because we were LVNs, we better not work because we needed to study. She twisted her face, lunged forward, clinched her eyes, and said in a firm, tough voice, "I'll put you out so fast, and you will never become an RN." I trembled at the intensity in her eyes because both of us had to work.

We continued working full-time, hoping she would not find out. She demanded money for different books on the spot and would not allow us to apply for any scholarships. She informed us that her husband supported those scholarships and would not be pleased if we were receiving any of the money. In obedience, I watched very little of the King marches until after graduation.

Sara confided with a nurse at work that she was not supposed to work while going to school. After working the 11-7 shift for a while, Sarah and the nurse applied to work the 3-11 shift; Sarah was chosen. The nurse was so angry she called the nursing school and reported that Sarah was working. The director was furious, and she put Sara out of school for working. The other students rallied around us. Marsha's husband had a friend who was a lawyer who offered to take the case, but Sara's mother had contacted the NAACP who got us back into class, and we graduated. They heard the entire story and wanted to act on it, but we just wanted to graduate. We did not want them to act on anything but our return to school.

After we marched in May, the nursing director told us we could not go to state board because we needed to repeat microbiology, which would not be offered until January. Subsequently, it would be one year before we could take state board of nursing exams. Refusing to let disappointment and the agony of defeat distract us, we waited and took the microbiology in January while working at County Memorial Hospital in La Marque.

With that accomplished, I was a full-fledged graduate nurse, so I could now officially wear my white uniform, along with the cap with the black stripe, instead of the striped uniform with the pinafore. When I put on the entire outfit, I felt like Ruby Jean, my first role model, and Julia, the nurse on television played by Diahann Carroll.

I moved to Houston and transferred to MD Anderson, shared an apartment with Brenda, and experienced another level of independence. We split the rent, groceries, and gas bill for my car. Coming from a background where bills were not paid on time, I insisted that we pay our obligations ahead of time. I valued being dependable, and I wanted good credit.

It gave me a sense of pride to place the rent in the hands of the manager ahead of time. Vivid memories from home of the rent man coming and knocking on the door to collect the rent when my parents did not have it made me cringe. Humiliated, Daddy or Momma, depending on who was available, respectfully pleaded, "Give me to next week. I'll pay it"

The rent man issued a warning, "You got to pay on time, or I have to make you move. You better have it next week. Yes, sir, I understand."

I felt sad that my parents had to take those kinds of threats, so I secretly vowed to buy them a home when I got to be a registered nurse. I wanted to avoid that predicament, therefore paying the rent on time was the right thing to do.

Finally, when June arrived, Sarah, Brenda, and I were apprehensive as to whether something else would delay our registration to take the board of nursing examination. The director sent in the paperwork, and we took the exams. We had to wait to get our scores through the mail although the school received its notification earlier. I called home and asked my mom had I received a letter from state board, and she said, "Yes, you have a long brown envelope, but you know I don't open your mail." I pleaded and tried to cajole her to open it, but she would not budge.

Sara left work and traveled to La Marque to get my grades. She called me at work and told me I made 92 and above on four of the tests, but my favorite, which was Psych, I made only 70. I squealed with delight and told all of my coworkers I passed state boards. Sara was petrified because I excelled in Psych and only made 70. She brooded, "What did I make?" The next day she got her grades and did well in four of them and made 71 in Psych.

We were elated that now we were permitted to write those coveted RN initials after our names. I experienced unparalleled joy that lifted my self-esteem to an unbelievable state of serenity, devoid of hurt and overflowing with forgiveness. We drove to the school to submit our paperwork and thanked the director for admitting us into the program; otherwise, LVN would have been my destination.

I could not have been prouder of my achievement and was so grateful we had overcome monumental psychological milestones. Weeks later it did dawn on me that we were the first blacks to graduate from the nursing program. The mold was broken; we paved a way and left a trail for others. I was headed toward new directions.

On a frequent basis, Sara, Brenda, and I talked about what happened to us, and even nowadays when we occasionally get together for lunch, we revisit and analyze the humiliation and rejection. We laugh at some of the hurdles but always point out we achieved what we set out to do.

Embarrassment was a powerful negative emotion that left imprints in different parts of my soul. Not necessarily all negative either. What I did not understand in my young formative years was that my spiritual strength, as my mother had taught me to depend on, empowered me to stand steadfast and not cry outwardly, just as Daddy had trained me. That inner strength allowed me to take insults and harsh treatments without incurring permanent damage to my soul and spirit or becoming incapacitated.

As a result, when I received a blow below the belt that knocked me down, I was able to get up off the canvas. Like most humans, I did not enjoy those painful experiences. I used my dad's humor template to tickle me to a functioning level. It gave me the dignity and a peace that I needed to stay focused, study, and learn. The two years of coarse treatment at Alvin Junior College paled in comparison to the thrill of victory that I attained with my RN designation.

My next goal was to work in the emergency center (EC) at Ben Taub Hospital where I could help critically injured and sick people. So I resigned from MD Anderson. Ironically, my many emergency room visits for asthma attacks is where my affinity for emergency nursing evolved. The opportunity to be at the hub of excitement with a medical team to save lives was a lofty goal for an inexperienced nurse. I applied for the job, prayed, and was hired. There was no orientation; I was told to come to work. My first night on duty, I was the only RN, with one LVN, an orderly, two clerks, and a utility aide.

As soon as the shift started, a buzzer sounded, which indicated that a patient was on the way to the shock room (where the most critical patients are placed). When I ran wide eyed and bushy tailed into the shock room, the doctor screamed, "Get the damn defibrillator." But I had no idea what he was referring to. He cursed and improvised until finally the LVN came with the defibrillator. He was so angry with me, and no matter how I explained that it was my first tour of duty, he levied epithets. Alas, I was initiated into the world of emergency room nursing.

This fast-paced environment, with emotions running high and critical patients to beholden my skills, forced me to quickly adapt and learn. It was a far greater soulful experience that I had imagined. A few weeks on duty, an asthmatic patient came in, and the doctor gave her some adrenalin subcutaneously, 50cc of aminophylline straight into the vein (IV push), and she vomited and gasped for breath as she wrestled with a pounding heart rate. I was keenly aware of what she was encountering as I had personally experienced that treatment many times.

I sought out the physician in charge and pleaded for a change in protocol. By diluting aminophylline 50 to 100cc of D_5W (5% dextrose in water) and letting it drip, the severe nausea and the tachycardia would be reduced. He was reluctant to do it at first, but after convincing him of personal experience of wrenching, vomiting, and bounding heart rate, he agreed to let me try it. Diluting the aminophylline in 100cc of normal saline became the standard protocol.

As a staff nurse, my favorite job was working in the EC on the 3-11 shift where there were multiple opportunities to work with the most critical patients. The blood, sweat, and tears gave me an emotional high that I just simply craved. The experience gave me a sense of gratitude because I was in a position to care for the sickest patients that came through the doors.

Nursing was everything I had dreamed of and more. I talked about it so much that my family said, "You sure love that place." I happily chanted, "Yes, I do." I thought I would never leave the EC, but as I grew and matured in the profession, my vision expanded, and my goals changed shape.

Sadly, Daddy died four months after being diagnosed with lung cancer. He did not know he had it nor did he suffer. I played a game of dominoes with him the day before, and that night he slipped away in his sleep. I was surprised when I got the call. He was supposedly expected to live a year. My dad, a proud man, died in dignity.

I got married that same year. At work I changed to the day shift, which did not give me the same level of excitement because there were fewer shock rooms. So I transferred to critical care.

Leadership Point

Round Two

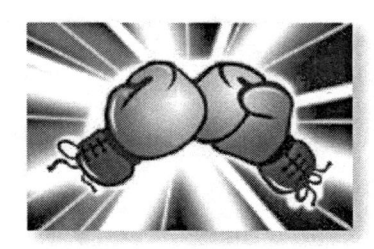

Study your opponent before you get in the Ring

1. Anticipate how you will respond to rejections, disappointments etc.
2. Recognize the kind of punches needed to subdue or abate the opponent.
3. Don't rely solely on past successes; individualize your approach.
4. Be prepared spiritually, psychologically and physically.
5. Expect to win.

CHAPTER 3

Training Camp

BOXERS GO TO training camp for conditioning, gaining stamina and acquiring skills so they can be fit and ready to win the match. Training is dependent upon the bout and how long it takes to become a champion. Not that all boxers become titled champions. But at the same time, they recognize that the best way to prepare is to step into the ring and box. That is similar to my entrance into leadership. I loved working as a staff nurse and attempted to do a good job. I volunteered for difficult assignments and took the lead on special projects.

Working in the coronary care unit spurred my interest in heart diseases and became my love. I liked Pinkie, my supervisor, and Ginger, my head nurse, and all the people I worked with. My work buddies, especially Dale, teased and called me a flunky because I did work that was not on my job description nor did I get paid for it. I experienced joy in what I was doing; therefore, I did not take their needling and small quips to heart.

I was widening my experiences and increasing my skill level, not with the intent to move into a management or leadership role, but because I enjoyed challenges. However, Mrs. Payton, a supervisor of clinics, noticed my work and asked me if she could submit my name for a head nurse (nurse manager) in the clinic. Of course I was enthused to be asked and thought I'll try it although I did not have any experience. This was my chance to get into the ring. My name was submitted, but Mrs. Payton informed me that my application was not accepted. A few weeks later a friend from Medical Arts Hospital told me they were looking for a head nurse and suggested I apply. I applied, was accepted, and resigned from Ben Taub.

Working at Medical Arts Hospital as a head nurse on the VIP floor gave me a chance to put on my boxing gloves and experience using different punches. The staff was accommodating and easy to work with, but many of the doctors did not accept me in the leadership role. I was the first black head nurse. They communicated with me through the clerk and nurse assistants. When they made rounds on the floor, I went bed to bed with them and often the patients gave commendations of how well they were treated and that I checked upon them to ensure they were satisfied.

The doctors seemed to ignore the compliments and the accounts that patients were satisfied with their care. One day, a doctor had stuck a patient twice while attempting to start an intravenous line (IV). She was hollering and screaming, "No more! Get somebody else!"

I was skilled at starting IVs; she needed it, so I asked her to let me try. If I did not get it on the first try, I would not stick her again. She agreed, but the doctor walked out of the room. I located a vein; the IV was started, and the patient's anxiousness subdued. The doctor never thanked me or mentioned it, but I noticed he began to say a few words to me when I gave him an update on a patient.

This was an indicator to me that even when you are not accepted, you don't get bogged down in rejections; you let your work speak for you. I recognized my job was to ensure the delivery of excellent care, so I focused on patient care outcomes to ensure there were no complaints about the management of the unit. In addition, I cultivated good relationships with the employees.

I worked at Medical Arts for nine months when one morning around 6:00 a.m. I received a call from Mrs. Moore, the director of nursing at Ben Taub, that the head nurse job in coronary unit was available. If I were interested, I could have it.

I was enjoying my role at Medical Arts, but I was happy to go home. When I submitted my resignation letter, Ms. Kyle wanted to know if there was anything wrong. I explained it was my dream to return to Ben Taub someday; however, I did not anticipate this offer. She accepted and asked me to attend the executive dinner board meeting, an invitation that had not been extended before. I was reluctant but reminded myself of my leadership obligations.

At the end of the meeting, I was given a certificate for providing good leadership, and I was surprised. My supervisor announced to them that I was resigning, and a couple of the physicians asked what needed to happen to make me stay. I declined because my heart was at Ben Taub, and no offer or good deed would change my mind.

I was excited to come back to Ben Taub, my employer of choice, in a management role. The head nurse job was a lot of work, but because I knew the people and had worked with them as a staff nurse, my adaptation was not too difficult. The supervisor, Mrs. Kackley, was friendly but micromanaged my unit. I had to learn a new skill in order to get along with her.

LEADERSHIP POINT

Round Three

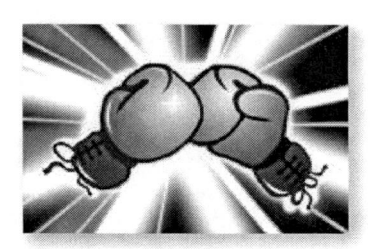

Upper Cut Disappointments

1. Counteract strong emotional residue with power punches.
2. Clear your head and refocus on your goal.
3. Avow to overcome impediments and roadblocks.
4. Take purposely planned steps to help you stay on your feet.
5. Weave back to the positive when the mind bobs to the negative.

CHAPTER 4

Featherweight

THE TRAINING I acquired at Medical Arts was a great beginning, but I recognized that I had to read some leadership books and go to management seminars to become an efficient manager (a champion!). In those days there were no management academies or management classes that managers were required to complete in order to prepare them for their roles.

My supervisor had years of experience, was a good communicator, and she managed like a maverick. The management structure for the head nurse role was limited, and by design the supervisor had a lot of input and control in the day-to-day operations. The best way to get the opportunity to run my unit was to work and plan ahead so she could see I was on top of things. Sometimes it worked; other times it didn't. So I savored the wins and got through the others. Over the years I received good evaluations. Prior to Mrs. Kackley's resignation, she commended me that I had achieved the experience and skills to be promoted.

Having only an associate degree in nursing, I needed a bachelor's degree. When I shared my plans with my mother and sisters they could not understand why I kept pushing myself. Since I was already an RN, what else did I need? Silvia, a friend who was a teacher and high on degrees, really encouraged me to do it. Ellis, supportive without hesitancy, encouraged me to do what I desired.

Another indicator that I needed a bachelor's degree was when the patient education instructor position was available and I applied but was told by Mrs. Frazier, director of nursing, that I did not have a degree. Therefore, she hired the degreed candidate. I clearly understood and decided never again would lack of a degree be an impediment in my career. So I returned to school in 1974.

Texas Woman's University (TWU) was in the medical center and in walking distance, so I chose it. Stemming from my experience at Alvin Junior College, I positioned myself in anticipation for the same at TWU. To my amazement, it was 180 degrees different. Hard work and good grades were respected. The instructors included me in class participation, and I was treated fairly. In an environment that was free of humiliation and embarrassment, I gained a thirst for knowledge.

Married, mother of a four-year-old son, Chuck, and working full-time in the ICU, I embraced the curriculum with the intent to master it. Some friends who had associate degrees or diplomas in nursing vowed they would not get a bachelor's degree in nursing. The requirements were strenuous in that you could only challenge two of the nursing courses; the others, including clinical had to be repeated. I was a five-year experienced nurse but had to go back to making beds and getting medicines as simple as milk of magnesia checked off by my instructors while using medication cards. Yet in the evening I went to work in a critical care unit where I was in charge.

In my friends' opinion, it was not worth it. I reminded them that according to the literature, if RNs did not have a bachelor of science degree in nursing (BSN) by 1985, they would be reclassified to registered nurse technicians. Fortunately, 1985 came and went and that never happened.

I was not elated with what I had to go through to get a BSN but that was what was available if I wanted one. I wanted one; thus, I got up off the canvas and figured how to get it done.

I continued to work full-time and go to school for the next two years. My employer, like most, did not alter schedules too often to meet my school demands, so I worked every weekend for a year so I could complete the clinical courses. One point of emphasis I consistently kept in the forefront was that my job came first. I stretched myself to another level using creative energy to develop new projects and get staff involved. The supervisor keenly watched to determine if going to school or the asthma affected my work. When I got my evaluation, she mentioned that my work and attendance remained at a high level and was excellent.

Through creative manipulations, I maximized my time to accomplish my goals. I went to the library so frequently Chuck considered it a playground. Subsequently, each time I picked him up from school, he asked if we were going to the library. Driving home from school, I listened to tapes, and Chuck often said, "Momma, do we have to listen to Herzberg again?" I explained that it was the only way I could get all of my lessons done. He often said, "I don't want to go to college if I have to study that hard."

When I attended Chuck's Little League games, I took an umbrella and a card table to use while I cheered and studied at the same time. I rarely missed a game. I was a den mother for five years and trekked to all of the Boy Scouts' outings. On vacations, a self-made plywood lap desk covered half of the backseat and provided me a table to write papers and still participate with the family. Ellis ran the errands and did most of the cooking. Grocery shopping was accomplished by driving my niece Kim and nephew Derek to the store, giving them a list to do the shopping while I remained in the car to listen to tapes and read.

When they got to the checkout counter, one of them came and got me, and I went into the store and wrote the check to pay the bill. Working on Sunday mornings forced me to church on Sunday nights. That old home training of giving the Lord priority in my life has always resonated in the line of what's important in my life.

Like a boxer who says, "Forget about what round you are in and win it," if I start focusing on "I am in round two, and I am so tired I can't see how I am going to get to the fifteenth round," it becomes insurmountable. But one round at a time is manageable. In other words, I keep my mind on the prize. That is what I would tell myself as I repeated each of those clinicals.

Eventually, 1976 rolled around, and I was ready to graduate, but there was a glitch. My advisor informed me that I had taken the wrong nutrition course, and immediately negative memories sought their way into my mind. I told her I had papers where they signed off on the nutrition course that I had taken. I retrieved the paper and brought it in the next day. She made a copy of it and told to me to check back after lunch. Upon return my problem had been resolved, so my heart rate returned to normal, and again I pushed the negative memories back into oblivion.

My family and friend Sylvia attended the graduation in Denton, Texas. When I walked across the stage to receive my diploma, I was happy until I looked inside of the envelope, and it said, "Report to the administration office." Once again I queried, "Is something wrong?" I sustained my poise until the ceremony was over. I then made a beeline with the family in tow to the administration office.

When I got there my tachycardia and high respiratory rates were noticeable as I relayed the problem to the clerk. She informed me that my name was misspelled, and they had to reorder the diploma. She handed me the reprinted diploma. I examined and read it to be sure it was authentic. When we got in the car, all of us began laughing that the emotional stress almost overshadowed our joy.

On return to work the following Monday, coworkers and staff were curious to know if I would be signing my name *Mary Holt Ashley, RN, BSN*. I continued the same designation of RN. My interest in management and leadership increased, and I was intrigued at learning how to get people to want to work.

LEADERSHIP POINT

Round Four

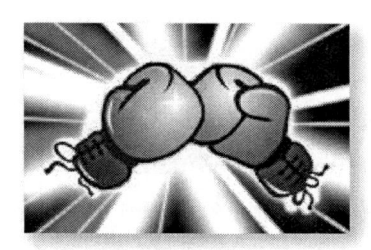

Jab Away Doubts

1. Position your mind, spirit and soul to the positives.
2. Confront doubts openly.
3. Get off the ropes and get started.
4. Humor yourself.
5. Revisit battles that you have won and enjoy the triumph.

CHAPTER 5

Featherweight Champion

ALTHOUGH I WAS at the featherweight level in management, I did not become a featherweight champion until I got a degree and engaged in creative work right along with required work. I volunteered to teach the EKG component of the critical care courses, and everybody was amazed that I was involved in education and taking on the head nurse role at the same time. My supervisor warned me that my first responsibility was to my unit, and I assured her there would be no neglect.

I developed a cardiac rehab program that caught the eye of the physician director of cardiology. It was the first time I initiated a project that involved multidisciplines. I talked to others, and it became a buzzword. The physicians agreed it was a good beginning but thought it should be separate from CCU with a nurse managing it. Since it was my project, I assumed I would be heading it but was told I would remain the head nurse, and another nurse would be responsible for the rehab portion. Although I was recognized for initiating the idea and that was a plus, I was disappointed and angry.

I did not share those feelings with anyone even though I was approached by other nurses who felt I had been dealt a raw deal. Instead of staying on the canvas, I got up, swollen eyes, sniffling nose, and a foggy head. I punched and punched the disappointment and anger out of my spirit. I admit the blow was hard; thus I even contemplated never getting into the ring again.

But deep down in my heart I knew the only way to become a champion was to jump right back into the ring. The clutter of negative thoughts was tossed into the cerebral hemisphere for transformation into an intellectual plan rather than an emotional blanket. I focused on discovering other ways to enhance and improve nursing.

Getting myself and staff involved in something exciting and challenging, I felt energized, connected, and valuable; the hurt and disappointment dissipated. After reading several articles about SOAP charting, I felt it would help strengthen the nurses' assessment and evaluation. The *S* stood for subjective symptoms, the *O* for objective symptoms, the *A* for assessment, and the *P* the problem. This process prompted nurses to include significant information in their charting that would benefit the physician in deriving a more complete overview of the patient. I sent a proposal to my supervisor that I wanted to initiate it in my unit. She approved but told me I also had to get approval from the chief of surgery, and that was a major impediment.

He told me I was trying to get nurses to act like doctors; therefore, SOAP charting was out of nurses' scope of practice. According to him, nurses did not have authority or skill to make those kinds of decisions. I respectfully disagreed and challenged him that it was going to happen because it was a standard for nursing practice. He still would not budge and said the doctors were not going to read all of that charting. Years later he became chief of staff and reminded me of our long ago, professional head butting.

The education department joined me in my quest, and finally, a year later, administration allowed me to pilot SOAP charting on my unit for six months. During the pilot period, Joint Commission on Accreditation of Healthcare Organizations (JCAHO) visited, and when they reviewed a patient's chart from CCU, they were impressed with the SOAP charting and recommended that it become a practice throughout the hospital. That was my turning point in the featherweight division.

As a super featherweight, I had accomplished a major change that impacted our nursing practices, and I was now a champion. In leadership roles, it is necessary to go beyond the job description. Never be stymied by your rank. I learned that good strategies can be initiated by any level of management as long as you are willing to step outside of that box and punch and punch until your goal is reached.

Mrs. Pecot, the critical care supervisor for the day shift, informed me she was resigning to move to another city with her husband and wanted to recommend me for her job. I was caught off guard because I knew there were 3-11 and 11-7 supervisors who wanted to come to the day shift. I was flattered by her asking me to let her put my hat into the ring knowing there would be a battle. When the interviewing process began, there were speculations as to who was deserving or who should get the job. One morning I overheard a remark that was unsettling.

I had gone to nursing administration to put in a schedule-change request, but all of the night and day supervisors were in the conference room for morning report. I waited outside of the room for someone to come out and sign my request. When the meeting was over, the supervisors began to discuss who was going to get Mrs. Pecot's position. Someone remarked, "I know Ashley applied and can do the job, but with all that wheezing, she should not get it."

The next week I was appointed as Pecot's replacement, wheezing and all. Pleased and eager to be on the team, I began immediately to erase those mean comments out of my head and set out to unite with the existing team. Things were going smoothly; then my asthma went to another level, and the doctor started me on high doses of prednisone. Within three months my dress size 7 ballooned to a 16 and in six months to a 20. I was devastated.

There were people who were bold enough to walk up to me and say in a teasing voice, "How did you let yourself gain all that weight?" or "You used to be such a cute size. What happened?" If I went into the cafeteria, the ladies on the serving line made jokes such as, "You don't need but a little piece of chicken," or "I'm not going to fill your bowl up. You are too fat." The unintentionally rude comments were like electrical volts discharging down my spinal cord. Amazingly, my spirit was resilient.

Some family members frequently were equally insensitive in their remarks such as, "I never would have thought you would be fat," or "You are fatter than Barb [older sister]." My eternal thanks to Ellis who never said a negative word about the weight gain. Dealing with my weight took a toll on my self-esteem. My eating was out of control partly due to the ravenous appetite, a side effect, imposed upon me by the use of high doses of steroids. I struggled to maintain a psychological balance with my physiological and physical responses. In spite of the stress, I stayed focused on my job and school.

Everything happens for a reason. I bumped into Dr. Awe, a pulmonologist with whom I had worked in the emergency room and had not seen in two years. I knew he saw the weight gain, but he did not mentioned it, so I gave him a full account of my status and asked him if I should get off the prednisone. He replied, "Holt, forget about what the damn people are saying. If your breathing is better, then to hell with them. I treat a lot of patients with prednisone, and they do not experience a change in their asthma."

That conversation was a springboard. I dragged myself up off the canvas and began to appreciate my physiological outcomes and started to work on my physical size. I achieved some weight loss, but losing weight was a struggle for me and has continued to be over the years.

Leadership Point

Round Five

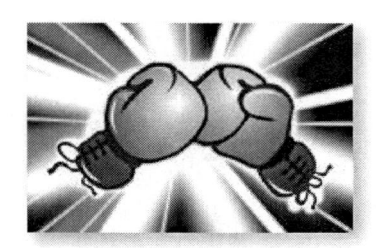

Fight One Round at a Time

1. Recognize that success is often achieved in steps.
2. Stay focused on the current round.
3. Use a combination of punches to attain your goals.
4. Don't be stymied if you lose a round or two.
5. Regroup, recharge and readjust your plan.

CHAPTER 6

Super Featherweight Champion

SNAPPING MYSELF OUT of the rut was manageable as I delved into and sorted out new pathways. Supervisors were promoted to assistant director, and my span of control enlarged to include the medical, neurological, surgical, and coronary care intensive units. Included in the change was the addition of shared secretarial services. That was a step up, to have someone to answer my phone because we had no beepers or cell phones, only overhead paging. It was not uncommon for my name to be blasted over the public announcing system ten to twenty times a day.

My first order to myself was to get to know the head nurses and the physicians for each unit. Some of the physicians did not want to be bothered, and one even said, "I'll call you when I need you."

Recognizing that I was still in the featherweight division even though I moved to the super featherweight level within that division, I had not yet earned the championship. With the new experiences, it became apparent that my style of leadership and management could not be the mom-and-pop model that I had successfully used to get the support of the staff in the small CCU unit to deliver excellence in care. Boxers who become champions have a unique knockout punch, but they must be able to change and adapt depending on the opponent.

I remember a fight between Muhammad Ali and George Foreman where Ali was considered the underdog because Foreman was younger and had a powerful knockout punch. Ali did not use his toe-to-toe approach; instead he used the rope-a-dope (a style his supporters had little faith in), where he leaned against the rope and let Foreman punch and tire himself out, and then Ali used quick jabs to knock him out. His strategy worked. A critical step when changing to a different position is to recognize when something more is needed. Don't wait to get started; you won't know until you try. Risk taking is imperative.

During the 1980s, it took a lot of creative strategies to forge professional relationships with physicians because they held the power and possessed the authority that was well supported by hospital administration. Nurses were often disrespected, and there was a line drawn in the sand as to where you could step without being labeled insubordinate. It was difficult to raise the confidence of head nurses and supervisors who were management's first line of defense. Usually if a difficult situation arose between a doctor and a nurse, the doctor was inevitably perceived as being right. Nurses felt helpless and powerless as a result.

I believe that relationships are critical to achieving success with and through people. The interconnectedness brings about a sense of community and a taste of unity. To make this happen, I needed to be creative and patient in establishing trust and relationships. Start small and get to know the staff and physicians, then enlarge my strategy was my game plan. I wanted to have a one-hour in-house nurse and doctor educational presentation. Partnering to provide continuing education to the staff helps to show respect and teamwork. It was the first time this approach had been tried. Physicians usually did the teaching, and the staff attended. Determined that it would be a combined effort, I secured Dr. Sears's help.

He was reluctant because he was not sure how the doctors would respond, so I asked that he and I do it. Later that month he informed me that one of his residents had agreed to participate. The educational offering was well received by the staff, and it led to other collaborative in-house seminars.

Situations don't just resolve themselves by complaints and sidebar conversations. I proposed to my head nurses that each of them set up a meeting with their chief to establish regular meeting times. In this day and time, it is an expectation that this be done. In the '80s, it wasn't the case, and the head nurses were intimated out of their wits.

Coaching, pushing, and even interceding on some of their behalf helped to get the meetings going and opened up new channels in relationships, not perfect by any means, but a good beginning. Dr. Greenberg was amenable and met with us regularly, and we had support from him.

Culture does not change with one new approach. It evolves when one repeatedly punches and punches. Simply sitting on my hands waiting for something to happen was not my style. The importance of staff and physicians developing professional relationships was far too valuable to the medicine department's goal of delivering excellent care that is predicated on teamwork.

I met with the head nurses every other week for two hours, and we bonded, and overtime we matured into an effective team. We knew each others' weaknesses and strengths. The philosophy of achieving excellence was embraced, and we experienced joy in perfecting our practice and delivery of care. One of the features of the meeting was a twenty-minute in-service leadership provided by the head nurses and me on a rotation basis. It increased presentation skills, built confidence, and improved leadership knowledge.

At first they complained about it, but I would not concede on the issue, and it evolved into a bright spot for the meeting. Secretly, they competed and enjoyed the camaraderie and the recognition. It reminded me of "Buster's pecan game" from my childhood. Through our unique togetherness, we became and were referred to as the medicine team.

I was working on my master's degree in nursing at Texas Woman's University (TWU) and working full-time when I was promoted to assistant director. My span of control enlarged as other units were added to my responsibilities. When I started the master's program I encouraged Brenda and good friend Isaac to go also, and we studied together and had a great time. I wanted to be an expert clinician because I loved the pathophysiology of heart diseases. To my surprise, the courses did not lead to that. In the first course, Practice Oriented Nursing Theories (PONT), I wrote a lot of papers. In my opinion, this course did not correlate to my goal of becoming an expert clinician.

The next course was even less impressive to me because I wanted courses to help me to be an expert in cardiac nursing. I expressed this to Dr. Harmon who told me to try one more course, and if I still felt that way maybe I should not pursue a master's degree in nursing. In the next course, my interest began to pique as I learned the Neuman's systems model that was TWU's framework for nursing care delivery. It was a new way of looking at how nurses deliver care based on an acceptable framework for practice that resulted in maximum patient outcomes.

The number of papers to be written increased. Dr. Harmon counseled me about my writing style and encouraged me to improve if I wanted to make an A. During the Christmas break, I purchased books on writing styles and practiced and practiced. Upon return to class, on my first ten-page paper I made 97 out of 100.

Dr. Harmon called me in and wanted to know how I had achieved these results. I described my self-learning method, and she was impressed and commended me. My skill to write continued to grow, and I kept getting As on my papers. A few years after I graduated, Dr. Harmon invited me to speak to her class on how to improve formal writing style skills.

A change in my attitude toward the program occurred when my appreciation evolved for explaining how people interact, mature, and work while recognizing that there are many viewpoints. Learning the theories of motivation took me to another horizon. The excitement of this new approach grabbed me, and my philosophy of people moved to a new level. It became my weapon to get people moving. My approach to leadership and management took an upswing as the more I learned the more I put into practice. My staff often commented, "You want us to learn everything that you learn. But remember, we are not in school."

It was rewarding to share information and get them involved because in order to grow any environment, the staff has to appreciate new concepts. I helped them to understand the Newman's model as a framework for taking care of patients. I was falling in love with leadership; it penetrated my heart, yielding an unexpected joy as I earned my super featherweight championship title.

Kenn and I published our first article in a nursing magazine, which gave me some connection in the nursing community. That achievement was another step up in my journey. I encouraged two people from my staff to write an article for the nursing department nursing paper. At first they were apprehensive and felt it was too much work, but with coaching and side-by-side guidance they were successful.

My master's program required a thesis or professional paper. I chose to do the thesis because it gave me a nursing research background. For my thesis, I used Herzberg's theory of motivation as my framework to determine nurses' levels of job satisfaction. It intrigued me that he purported money was not a motivator and that there were other components of work that had more impact on employees doing a great job and loving it. Long before I was ready to collect data for my thesis, I began to employ some of his theory into practice. I wanted to test it to see if I was able to influence staff to get work done when I gave them meaningful work and allowed them to work it out.

My first attempt at gathering evidence to determine if giving an employee important work without increasing their pay would serve as motivator was tested on a clerk. Making out the time schedule was an arduous task that had an air of responsibility associated with being a manager. I believed that it was something that could be done and managed by a clerk. I asked Norma, if she was interested in learning to do the time schedule, and she was honored to make out the time and grant time-change requests, which gave her a level of authority.

Over a period she became excellent at it. Word soon got around that Norma was doing my work, and the other assistant directors were inquisitive as to how I got her to do it. Later that next year, timekeeping became a clerical job.

My passion for leadership spurred me to buy the latest books and study them, a habit I sustained during my career, and I continue to study in my retirement. I wanted to excel as a leader, so all my readings concentrated on leadership. My favorite journals are the *Journal of Nursing Administration* and the *Harvard Business Review*, but I have many books on a variety of leadership and management topics. Peers teased me about all the reading that I did and would often say, "Ask Ashley. I know she has read it."

The more I studied and practiced the theories and principles of leadership, the more I valued them. I was dazzled by the impact motivation had on employee productivity. It worked for them just as it worked for me when I was growing up when Dad got us to do work.

It was crystal clear to me that praise and recognition are powerful aspects in my leadership role. I developed an employee recognition program. The medical nursing department was the first and only department for many years to have Employee of the Year recognition programs. Each worker, nursing assistant, clerk, licensed vocational, and registered nurse had an Employee of the Year program and the option to compete to fulfill the requirements. My philosophy was that on a team all are of equal importance, and each has equal weight.

One essential criterion of each program was that the nominee demonstrated that he or she used a creative idea that was not part of the job description to enhance something related to patient care, the environment, or the employee. Helping employees to use all of their talents and skills is a great way of building confidence and maximizing employee's abilities.

The other criteria included points awarded for excellent time and attendance; a high annual evaluation score; letter of commendation from coworker, supervisor, another department, patient, family, or physician. These criteria when fulfilled have direct impact on productivity.

The nominations were reviewed and scored, and the person from each category of worker who received the highest score became the Employee of the Year. There was a public ceremony with administration, their family, staff, and physicians in attendance. The public recognition was a positive experience for the employees. Recognition has to be earned in order for it to be a motivator; therefore, it is important to challenge the employee to stretch.

The creation of the Physician of the Year award was a great relationship builder. Employees submitted the physician's name and described how he or she made a difference in patient care or employee relationships. The doctor who was judged the most compassionate received the honor. The award was presented at the department heads meeting and was well received. It strengthened the relationship between physician and staff.

While eating lunch in the cafeteria, Ruth commended me on being creative and for engaging in new ideas. I told her that I enjoyed it, but it is difficult for me to measure my creative potential because of the lack of resources. I will always wonder, "What could I achieve if I had a sufficient budget and strong administrative support?" Unfortunately, insufficient budgets can rob one's curiosity bank or make it difficult to apply your creativity to derive excellent outcomes. Yet the mystique and the challenge to explore and make something happen send the beta cells into overdrive as the adrenalin flows.

I published my first solo article in a refereed journal, the *Nursing Management Journal*, entitled "Getting the Medicine Units Going." It was based on the use of motivational strategies that produced changes in productivity, reduced patient complaints, and improved employee attendance. The acceptance of the article for publication in a refereed journal that potentially could be read in many states fostered a sense of personal accomplishment while promoted the hospital statewide.

It was worth the long hours spent writing the article at home because there was not time at work nor did administration support using work time to write articles. The importance of contributing to the profession of nursing through publishing is a worthy sacrifice for professional growth. On the other hand, sharing strategies and stories about our organization informs the public of it successes.

The first time I was asked to be a speaker at a seminar was at a statewide seminar for perinatal nursing where I spoke on motivation. I was challenged and pleased at the same time. I had presented in my own hospital environment but not to a large group of unfamiliar faces. I was now entering another phase of leadership—speaking before audiences. If I intended to be a champion, it was time to get in the ring and experience the punches and discover my own style.

Norma, a friend of the family, advised, "Just be yourself. Do not try to be Barbara Jordan or a Jesse Jackson." I trained and trained in preparation for my first big event. I visualized how I would look and how I would walk across the stage. I read books on how to prepare for a presentation, and many suggested that you put on the clothes that you are going to wear the day of the presentation and get in front of a mirror and practice. Being an amateur and willing to study, I followed those instructions.

I had no coach, but I remembered my parents' prodding from my youth speech-making days. Momma encouraged, "Pray so you won't get nervous." Daddy urged, "Step on that stage. Look them in the eye and show your stuff 'cause ya are ready to knock their socks off."

Both of their advice resonated with me as I walked onstage holding the transparencies in my hand. I did not have the luxury of a PowerPoint presentation, no such thing during this era. I used transparencies with the hope they were in the right order.

As I walked toward the stage, I dropped my transparencies, and they scattered everywhere. This is not what I had visualized. As I scrambled around picking them up, because they were slick, they stuck to the floor. I had to deliberately use my fingernails to pick each one up. Minutes were ticking off the clock, but it felt like hours. It forced me to come up with some quick humor to divert the audience's attention and quiet my frustrations.

I don't recall what I said, but I know that their laughing reduced my anxiety, and a sense of peace appeared. Finally, I got up off the floor and stood up with the transparencies in hand, and the audience gave me a standing ovation. Their applause energized me and restored my zest to do battle.

I approached the podium with confidence, and I got through the rounds noticing that each time I accomplished a round, my comfort level increased. I defeated my opponents: anxiety, embarrassment, and neophyte adequacy. That seminar carved the pathway for many more local and national speaking engagements.

Leadership is as much of an internal responsibility as it is an external one. I connected to other nursing and leadership groups as well as professional nursing organizations. I joined Texas Nurses Association and the Eta Delta chapter of Sigma Theta Tau and the Top Ladies of Distinction. I became an active supporter and remained in positions of responsibility.

Almost never turning down community or professional organizations when they asked me to speak or do work, my schedule was jam-packed most of the time, leaving little room for myself. Johnetta, my sister-in-law, frequently reminded me it's okay to say no because I was now being chosen to "erase the blackboard," and I didn't have to overdo it. She was alluding to my high school years when I yearned to be asked to do that task but was never chosen.

When administration decided to hire a director for the emergency and ambulatory services, I applied because I met the criteria: master's degree, proven track record, loyalty to the hospital, and previous experience as a staff nurse in emergency services.

Mr. Rollins interviewed me and told me I would be very competitive, and he would let me know after all the candidates were interviewed. Applicants had to be interviewed by several persons. A few weeks passed, and I encountered the human resource reviewer in the hallway, and he said one of the remarks about me was, "She is just like Jesus. There is no fault with her resume, but keep looking."

More weeks passed, and I saw one of the doctors on the committee who asked me what would happen if I did not get the job. My reply was, "If they find a candidate that has the same level of education and has experience as an emergency service director, I would understand. My personal belief is that the best candidate should be chosen."

Later, Virginia, a master's degree—prepared nurse with previous emergency services experience at the director's level, was hired. I accepted the decision as a fair one and continued to work at full speed in the medicine department, finding new opportunities and getting involved in new and exciting projects. I welcomed Virginia, and we sustained a professional relationship throughout her employment.

Administration decided to divide the hospital into three areas: emergency and ambulatory services, operative services, and inpatient services, with each having a vice president with presumed same level of authority. Anyone working during this era can vouch that there was a pecking order in the manner of authority and the allocation of resources: emergency and ambulatory, number one; operative services, number two; and inpatient, number three.

The differences were noticeably felt and expressed by nurses from the inpatient area. A lot of encouragement and positive recognition had to be provided to keep morale up among the inpatient staff as they observed and recognized the partiality. As a leader for the inpatient medical nursing department, I strategized to keep the staff focused on what they do and how it ties in to the overall picture.

All assistant director positions were upgraded to directors, and I became the director of medicine. My boss, Ms. Frazier, did not want those titles and fought against it because she felt that title would be misinterpreted, and directors would be viewed as the director of nursing in charge of the entire nursing department. After a series of meetings with Mr. Fairman, the deputy administrator for the district, all supervisors were upgraded, but we were instructed by Ms. Frazier to write your name and sign director, medicine, surgery, or pediatrics and not director of medicine. That signature did not bother me; I was happy and content to be promoted.

Leadership Point
Round Six

Get Up off the canvas before the count of ten

1. Expect knockdowns but don't wallow in self pity.
2. When you receive a blow; recoil quickly and go to the center of the ring.
3. Keep your eyes on the goal.
4. Compose your spirit to battle.
5. Refuse to look back instead keep punching.

CHAPTER 7

Middleweight Champion

UPON MY APPOINTMENT as director of medical nursing, I knew I had transitioned to another level of leadership and management. We were permitted to wear street clothes, but the suit became my signature dress throughout the remainder of my career. I learned that titles do count. As a featherweight, I performed like a champion and excelled like a middleweight contender but did not have the title. Reflections of why boxers who are excellent fighters strive so hard to attain the title became more transparent. Although you must work at championship level to qualify for the title, until you attain it you are not the recognized champion.

As a director, there is a level of respect you receive from others at meetings, groups, and in the community just because of your title. Your voice is more audible and should carry more authority; however, many times that did not happen to me. I had to fight and push my way in order to get some of my ideas across. Some doors would not open even when I had the right key, and some occasions when the door was open, I was present but not counted. This did not constrain nor detain; life experiences taught me not to let rejection chain me to the canvas. I spoke up and gave my idea or opinion, no matter the chill I felt. Overtime, some of my input was respected.

Even when you as a person are not accepted, if your work is superb and brings the expected outcomes, those who are narrow-minded sooner or later recognize the outcomes. As a leader I often whispered confidently to myself, *If you like my outcomes, then go ahead, be biased against me all you want. Just don't stand in my way of progress.* My experience in being in places where I was not wanted and accomplishing my goal in spite of it inoculated and immunized me so I could sustain the right attitude and the stamina to be productive when subjected to unpleasant situations.

In the midst of pursuing my master's degree, on Valentine's Day, my mother was rushed for emergency surgery to release adhesions from a previous surgery. She remained there for six months. Her illness, school, work, and family demanded a balancing act as I walked a tightrope. Nearing the end of her illness, after ten days of uncontrollable seizures that left her blind and brain dead, there was no hope.

I resigned that her earthly life was over, so I prayed, "Dear God, rescue her from this body." At first when I shared my prayers with my family, Barb, my oldest sister took me to task. Subsequently, as mom lingered, we all came to the same conclusion; hence, we united in prayer for God to release her from this misery.

The pressure was taking its toll on me. Three weeks before my comprehensive exams, Momma died on June 20. I flirted with the thought of dropping out of school but words paraphrased from the poem, "Don't Quit," inspired me:

> When things go wrong as they sometimes will
> When the road you're treading seems all uphill
> Rest if you must, but don't quit

After we survived the funeral, I took a week of vacation to study and prepare for the comprehensive exams. Always playing a "beat the clock" game as time evaporated, I wished for the power to turn back the hands to give myself more hours to study. The wish was not granted. I had to uppercut interruptions, jab away doubts, and counterpunch sleep as I battled the innumerable amount of materials I had to cover.

I passed the two-day written exam and was able to complete the remaining requirements for graduation. Fatigued and battle-worn, I stepped out of the ring with a master's degree, feeling perhaps like Joe Frazier felt when he defeated Muhammad Ali. Jubilant!

I did not attend graduation because I did not want to take any more time off from work to go to Denton. Completion of the master's degree in nursing administration further motivated me to encourage staff nurses and peers to get their bachelor's, master's, or go from being a nursing assistant to a licensed vocational nurse to an RN. After all, I had walked in those shoes. When employees complained that supervisors did not understand what it is to be a nursing assistant or licensed vocational nurse instead of a registered nurse, I shared with them my wonderful experience as a nursing assistant and LVN.

I emphasized, "My pathway was not easy nor is it the only way. But it was achievable, and each of you can do the same." I prided myself in accomplishing the feat. I further expounded, "When you love what you do, there is a joy that is created on the inside that no one can take away from you. That joy becomes your strength."

My encouragement to employees, "Be the best where you are, and be proud of the work that you do." I did not limit my words of encouragement to nurses but wherever I saw the need, which included other managers, housekeepers, parking lot attendants, transportation assistants, and so on. The joy that you experience from the work you do every day propels you to a high level of productivity.

I further explained, "Bloom where you are planted. Find your niche and look for opportunities to create something new and different in the role you are currently in and enjoy those outcomes." So often people squander their time not performing well right where they are without realizing that every day in the work environment they are carving out their work history.

If you want to further your career, the opportunity to advance a career is available. When you have aspirations for growth, take the first steps. Don't just dream about where you want to go. Get started. Over the years, a number of people reminded me that I role model those behaviors. My encouragement and prodding helped them to seek greater rewards in their work life.

Some earned degrees and got better jobs; others became more productive where they were and remained in the position. Their incremental accomplishments justified me taking the risk to broach the subject of upward mobility with employees while recognizing that some do not necessarily welcome intrusion into their personal territory. I have continued that practice in my retirement.

Leadership has to be studied and put into action. It does not matter how many degrees you have earned. It is essential to success in your leadership role that you continue to study leadership by way of seminars, professional journals, latest leadership books, and professional groups. Otherwise your ideas and ways of doing become stagnant and irrelevant. Sometimes you hear or read the same thing over and over again with a different flair. That's no different than attending Bible study where you hear the same lesson repeated, but your level of maturity helps you to discern truth better, and you gain new insight. A fresh perspective is a catalyst to new ways of doing, whereas stagnation keeps you stuck in the rut of tradition, thus getting the same old results.

Once I attended a Dale Carnegie leadership seminar where again interpersonal relationships were the topic of choice. The lecturer drew a pie on the blackboard and began to engage the class in discussion. He asked, "What is the most important factor in leadership?" I, a newly master's degree-prepared leader, eagerly held my hand up and responded, "Education." He drew a division in the pie, but it was only a small slice. I felt a little huffy but decided I needed to listen and learn.

Several other participants named factors that received small slices also. Then he carved a slice covering half of the pie and labeled it "interpersonal relationships." I knew it was important but did not realize its position in the food chain of leadership characteristics. He expounded on the need to know your employees and have a relationship with them because they are your most important resources. The more he explained the concept of interpersonal relationship, I saw its correlation to motivation and productivity.

It triggered my mind to ask myself, *If I don't know what makes my employees tick, how will I successfully set the tone for motivation to occur?* A virtual pie was embedded into my mind to remind me that half of what I do must be centered on relationships with my employees. That concept served me well throughout my career, and it became one of my knockout punches.

Unfortunately, employees do not fall into a one-size-fits-all category. There are personal and professional relationships that I cultivated with my employees because I needed both. They need to know that I smile, laugh, and cry just like them. I shared the same hobbies, career aspirations, and even childhood stories.

During this time, I was a staunch Dallas Cowboy fan. I watched all of their football games and was well grounded in each player's stats and gingerly admired Coach Landry as a leader. Being football smart gave me something to chat about with male employees; thus there was an easy connection that helped me establish relationships.

Over the years, I learned a lot about many employees' children; therefore, it seemed as if we were actual next-door neighbors. Being in touch with my employees was a source of strength that helped me deal with issues and problems with a sense of confidence that I could depend on their support.

Some nursing assistants envied LVNs, and they envied the RNs who in turn had ambivalent feelings about management. It is often a circle of disharmony that can disrupt the work environment if a concerted effort is not made to raise the consciousness that a unit is team dependent on each member to achieve work outcomes. Individual team members often perceive that they are the underdogs and are not important.

Knowing the full ramification of such experiences, I intentionally focused attention on areas to help employees feel inclusive while recognizing that they also must feel good about their roles. When I made rounds on the unit, I often alternated rounding with the nurse assistants and the nurses to tell me about their patients. Many times if they were making beds I would get on the other side and help finish the bed.

Frequently, I engineered opportunities for the nursing assistant or LVN to take the lead on an assignment and present it at my department head meetings. One strategy that raised self-esteem was to have one of them review a new policy and procedure and explain it to the nurses. This strategy helped demonstrate that each member, regardless of job status, was valuable to the team.

Helping head nurses to embrace the power of motivation was a laborious task as they often felt that they were too busy doing their work to plan and implement motivational strategies. It was of great importance to help the managers understand that motivation is both intrinsic and extrinsic. They tended to use the extrinsic type more often because it relies on some external reward.

Intrinsic motivation appeals to the sense of purpose, passion, and inner feelings; thus it is more time consuming. Effective motivation comes from being inspired. My coaching and continuous education along with role modeling began to pay off as the nurse managers put into practice simple strategies, which grew over time.

Vernice was the first to discover that making a bulletin board with all of her staff's pictures and names on it drew staff attention, and there was a sense of pride. It was a morale booster, and it helped patients and physicians to remember their caregiver's name. It was cost effective and employee-centered. Motivational strategies don't necessarily have to be expensive. Accustomed to being frugal due a limited budget and having no money during childhood days, I impressed on the managers the value of excelling with what they had.

Sharing and repeating successful outcomes was big on my list long before benchmarking became a buzzword. When something worked well in one area, the other units were encouraged to try it. They implemented it, adding their own twist.

To further understand employees in my department, I developed an employee satisfaction survey. The questions were designed to solicit information that employees usually won't share in open meetings. The instrument was not standardized nor did it have established reliability and validity; however, the information was great for annual goal setting and developing strategies. I shared the findings with my head nurses and my boss. Over the years, long before there was a hospitalwide employee survey, this data was referenced in describing employee behavior.

As I continued to focus on employee relationships, I purposely worked on changing characteristics about myself. I had employees say to me, "You don't smile, so you look mean, but you are nice." I needed to do better, so I talked a lot so employees could see the real me. Another thing, I placed a mirror on the back of my desk nameplate. As I talked to employees who came into my office, I could watch my body language and smile so as not to give off a negative impression. This practice was followed until I retired.

I engaged in interactions with employees at all levels and got to know them and their families. There is no greater reward to your employee than for the leader to be supportive when unforeseen events or special occasions arise.

If there was a death in an immediate family, I attended the funeral and offered words of encouragement. Church services, weddings, graduations, and other personal employee events received my attention and support. I enjoyed them and appreciated the diverse cultural lessons that evolved overtime as I continued to expand my cultural horizons.

Working with staff from the Philippines, India, Africa, Vietnam, China and other cultures increased my skill set in cultural diversity. The opportunity to build nurturing relationships with people of different backgrounds was a highlight of my career. I read literature and attended workshops on diversity to increase my awareness as I cultivated a strong work environment that was inclusive and culturally sensitive.

My level of accountability as a director was greater both internally and externally. I was responsible for firing employees. As head nurse, supervisor, and assistant director, I recommended firing, but now the buck stopped with me. Recommending firing and actual firing are two different acts impacted by psychological, social, and spiritual factors.

My first firing experience was John, who had repeated absences and tardiness and thus had accumulated enough negative points to be terminated. The hospital had a defined point system that helped management determine the action to take against employees who had gained a certain number of points; thus, he was on final warning. A review of his records indicated that the head nurse had followed all the steps.

I called John into my office to review his records and have him tell me what he thought the outcome should be. He wanted me to give him another chance because he needed his job. He whined that school was getting ready to start, and his kids needed clothes. He would not address his reasons for not following the policy. I expressed my appreciation for his opinion and reminded him the number of opportunities he had been given to correct his record.

While I listened, he pointed the finger and assumed no accountability for his predicament. I suggested some changes that he needed to make in the future but informed him termination was in order. He began yelling and hitting the desk saying, "I need my job. I need my job." The office was small, so he frightened me, and I felt boxed in, but I contained my composure until he quieted down. I then called security to escort him out of the office. I vowed thereafter never to hold an anticipated firing in my office but always in a conference room, where there is more space for such a sensitive and potentially volatile activity.

The lingering thoughts of whether he would find a job in time before the start of school harbored in my mind throughout the day. I revisited my own feelings and emotions when I did not have new clothes at the start of school, and immediately a cloud of sadness floated before my eyes. "Oh my goodness, those kids will be so disappointed." I couldn't help but empathize.

As a leader I had to make the fairest decision, so I consoled myself that I had taken the appropriate actions. Once I got home I reviewed the pros and cons to see whether there was anything I could have done differently. I felt that I had handled it appropriately, and while there was no guilt on my part, I felt for his circumstances. Closure was my next step.

When a termination took place, rumor usually spread like a malignancy throughout the department and the hospital. Employees would ask questions, and my response was, "He is no longer employed, and the rest is confidential." His tearing and the pleading rung in my ears for a week or two, but I repeatedly reminded myself that I followed the policy, and opportunities for improvement had been extended. My source of peace was in knowing that the right thing had been done. Boxers have to keep punching even when their pain is almost unbearable, so I managed my pain.

The director's role allowed me to get involved in community meetings where I soon discovered as I sat at the table with leaders from other hospitals in the medical center that Ben Taub did not have the respect it deserved. Again, in a familiar spot, I knew how to deal with the situation at hand.

The county hospital, overshadowed by our counterparts in the medical center, was often viewed by many as being less capable of delivering excellent care. In fact, to the contrary, millions of miracles occurred within the walls of our organization, and patients attested to their satisfaction.

I had to be aggressive in establishing who we were and to help demystify preconceived ideas of inferiority. This enduring process got better over my thirty years in leadership at the district. I believed in the district's mission and vision, and I knew that our goals and aspirations were the same for our patients and employees as other hospitals. We passed the same inspections and audits from regulatory agencies and received some of the same recommendations for improvements as most hospitals did.

Establishing an institution's identity is not lip service. No matter how many times I verbally defended the district, seeing the evidence was the only way to change mind-sets. I established partnerships with other nursing departments on special projects and invited them into our facility to observe our products and the way we do business.

Several staff members served on different external collaborative committees to increase our visibility. For sure, if you are not at the table you cannot be counted. Most often, what people in the community thought they knew about the district was only what the newspapers reported.

Negative stories reporting overcrowded emergency rooms, long waits, and accounts that people who came for services were treated badly from a customer service perspective and from lack of proper medical care were long-standing. The sixty- to seventy-seven-bed wards limited patients' privacy and often led to overblown legends being circulated. Such circumstances coupled with a book called *The Hospital*, written by Jan De Hartog in 1965 about Jefferson Davis hospital, set up a veritable Mount Rushmore of negative opinions that required long-term positive actions by leaders who believed and supported the vision and mission of the district.

Taking care of the poor and ensuring they receive the proper care may not be a suitable environment within which everyone can or should work. It was for me, however. Coming from an impoverished background, I connected immediately to the spirit of the poor, knowing intimately that their needs and aspirations were no different than any other class of people. I could passionately advocate those needs and work in collaboration with management to ensure they received excellent care.

During the 1980s, there were efforts to enhance customer service and ensure excellence in nursing care that was part of the strategic plan, but it was not driven by a financial commitment to make it happen. Budget cuts, long-standing insufficient staffing ratios, and a weak nursing voice resulted in inadequate resources to fully actualize strategic nursing plans. As I began to attend more internal administrative meetings, I fully understood why my nurse leader frequently denied budget requests from my department. She did not have the authority to make decisions because for the most part, what nursing received was handed down with very little input from nursing. Rarely was it sufficient for the inpatient units, whereas the emergency and operative services usually had what they needed.

Not having sufficient staffing for the medicine department did not keep me from forging my staff forward in a spirit of unity with a goal to make something happen. I had to deliver the bad news of no new positions and no pay increases, but I tempered it with compassion, respect of the employees' feelings, and a plan of action.

To panic and get the staff upset would only lead to more untoward consequences. In dealing with disappointments, I put on my best face, a pair of gloves, and entered the ring. Meeting with staff around the clock to explain the plan was never jolly times. Staff had to have their say, and it was necessary that I listen. I was careful in my choice of words so as not to alienate them, but I also recognized my role as a leader. Sometimes the fatigue from the meetings did not allow for discussion of the plan because airing of employee feelings became the only agenda item. That was okay because if employees were upset, they won't hear a thing I said.

Weeks after news of such dire magnitude have been delivered, throughout the building the mumbling and grumbling of unfairness was the topic of employee huddles. Rumors abounded. Special meetings were called to balance the misinformation and unfounded gossip and to disseminate the facts. Of course, facts alone do not automatically create happy employees, but they help set the tone for creating a plan of action.

Key factors for proper fact dissemination include the following: visibility of the leader, timing, good channels of communications, and follow-up meetings in small groups to thank employees for working through the challenges. I was careful to keep the meeting intact ensuring that the language was acceptable and that I did not placate the employees. Consciously, I focused on being a superb listener and drew out their concerns using a balanced approach of compassion and reality.

The will for surviving and thriving in the midst of challenges can stir up employees. It was imperative to get them involved as I tackled the issues. A sense of team effort evolved when all were involved. Having worked with them, I knew they had great ideas, and I valued their creativity. Staffing solutions in the face of hiring and wage freezes were dependent on staff ownership to help fix the problem.

My first steps included forming a team with representatives from each level of worker. When the input that was given was utilized and evaluated to the extent of its appropriateness, the staff enjoyed being on the change team. They became spokespersons for the strategy and helped diffuse some of the negative feelings and disappointments. Time and patience were virtues that I embraced as I dealt with this critical issue.

We created different divisions of work by identifying tasks and procedures that nursing assistants could perform to reduce the workload of the nurses. A few RN positions were converted to get two nursing assistant positions per RN, hence creating more people to do work.

The increase in procedures and additional responsibilities allowed us to increase nursing assistants' pay, which was more budget acceptable than adding new RN positions. I could have easily sunk to the canvas and given up; instead, I stood up and recognized that the work had to go on, and with the employees' help, the team would survive. This was a challenge, but it was an exciting time to take risks. Achieving through struggling and effectively grasping available resources is what I do best, and for me, growth occurs while I am trying to climb a mountain.

Would the nursing assistant see this change with more work, and would the plan prove effective? Experience taught me that ownership, participation from the ground up, and acceptance of good ideas no matter which level of worker gives the suggestion are key factors to making a plan work.

When the plan was ready to roll out, each team member presented it, and we received further input from other staff members. Agreement was reached, but major problems were encountered during the implementation phase. The manner in which each RN interpreted the use of nursing assistants was not consistent with the intended guidelines.

Some RNs were delegating every nonnursing task to the assistant even to the point of walking in the patient's room who needed the bedpan but having them wait until the nursing assistant was located. That attitude did not foster the team spirit or the customer service that was needed to accomplish the new structure. I had to go back to the drawing board to reassess the issues.

The most significant lesson learned from this project—when attempting to institute a major change, a brief discussion of how it is be implemented is not sufficient. The entire scope of the change process should be discussed and expounded. Additional classes essential for those involved included the following: attitudes in relationship to change, how to deal with difficult people, sustained commitment, and evaluation at different intervals.

Success in implementation of a change in practice is dependent on a well-organized and structured plan where all of the components are taught prior to starting the plan. Much of the frustration and misunderstanding occurred because staff was not well prepared.

I confessed to the staff that I did not prepare them well, and therefore additional training was needed. We started over with classes and more discussions, using the data we had gathered during the short implementation period. All of the employees had the training. Provided with the same information, employees' interpretations were clearer, and there was more commitment. What a difference it made, and the staff began to reunite, and within a year we were where we had expected to be.

Continuous encouragement and commendations helped to facilitate relationships. Team building, never cured by one act or strategy, is an ongoing process. It takes repetition and patience. On occasions there were flare-ups between the nursing assistants, but they were managed by the head nurse. New staff received the training from the education department prior to joining the staff on the unit. When a boxer loses a round and his spirit starts to wane he hangs closer to the ropes. Then something triggers his mind that he must continue to fight. He then repositions himself to the center of the ring indicating he is ready to fight. My boxing instinct led me to the center of the ring.

LEADERSHIP POINT

Round Seven

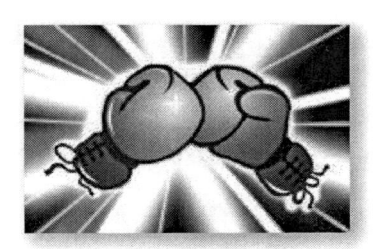

Fight with Dignity and Integrity

1. Facing each obstacle, opponent or situation with dignity and integrity places you in a position to deliver strong trustworthy punches.
2. Dignity and integrity characterize and differentiate a leader's identity.
3. Allow your values to dictate how you win a battle.
4. Be bold and confident not braggadocios and haughty.
5. Uphold the privilege of leadership.

CHAPTER 8

Super Middleweight Champion

IN JANUARY 1983, I checked out the new doctoral program at TWU. The semester had begun, but my curiosity prompted me to take a look at the curriculum. I had no intention of going for a doctorate. I picked up the information, and the following day got a call from Carol saying the class had just started, and that I could still register. She encouraged me to try the first class, so I registered, and the rest is history. I stayed the course. It was a major turning point in my life and career. Again I was working full-time as a nursing director, full-time student, wife, and mother.

I entered the super middle weight division—a different weight requirement for boxers and leaders. My weight of responsibilities ballooned to another level. I took on new opponents. My punches, stamina and agility were repeatedly tested. I vowed to be a champion—not just a contender.

This time around, I hired a weekly housekeeper. A former domestic worker, I was determined not to treat my housekeeper as a persona non grata. I tried a series of people until I got Martha who became a friend of the family and performed her work in an exceptional manner. We talked about our children, our faith, *The Young and the Restless* soap opera, and many other things. She was dependable, honest, and initiative.

Friends and relatives bonded with her, and I honestly felt that my previous personal experiences as a maid, negative as they may have been, prepared me to be a boss that was congenial and loving to her while expecting high work ethics. Reflective thinking helps me to fortify that I can pluck nuggets from any situation that can be used to help me be a better person.

Getting back into the academics, the new learning environment, friends, and professors sparked excitement and new energy into my career. Being the first students in the program, we took several courses that were later changed as the program continued. The challenge of research, writing, and achieving excellent grades were like ribbons on a gift waiting for me to open them.

Research and statistics, new endeavors, were intimidating Goliaths, but David slew the giant with a slingshot so I mumbled to myself, *Get out your slingshot and go for it.* The courses were difficult, but I mastered all of them. Admittedly, it took me awhile to get the hang of statistics, and by and large, I owe that success to Betty Henderson who helped me get on board with the statistics and the computerized components.

Working on a doctorate did not arouse any long, inquisitive dialogue among friends. By now my reputation for going to school was well established. Most of them shrugged their shoulders and asked, "What will you do with it?" In a sense I understood their argument because I was well grounded in hospital nursing leadership and had no desire to become a professor or a researcher.

Leadership jobs and roles in hospitals barely required a bachelor's at that time, and I was already master's degree-prepared. So what was my goal? The truth is it was my internal drive to achieve my own personal excellence. Few people understand that intrinsic needs surpass external ones more often than they are willing to admit.

My biggest fear was getting permission from my boss to go to class at 1:30 p.m. on Tuesdays and Thursdays. Mrs. Frazier was nice and not hard to deal with though she did not want anything to interfere with me working eight hours a day. So she agreed that I could work 5:30 a.m. to 1:15 p.m. on class days.

To show my appreciation, I did not take any unscheduled vacation or sick days the whole year. Keeping my work record in top-notch shape was as important to me as going to school; subsequently, I persevered. Despite the grueling hours I developed closer relationship with the 11-7 shift staff which was a win-win situation.

By the time our class of thirty-three was ready to take the statistics qualifying exam, the number of students had dropped considerably. We had to make 90 percent on the test to qualify, proceed with writing the dissertation proposal, and take the other courses. The manual exam consisted of ten statistical problems that filled at least four of the blue test taking booklets.

I only worked nine of the problems, which meant I had to get them all right. For three weeks, waiting for the scores from the Denton campus, I had nightmares of not passing. I absolved myself in projects at work to muzzle the unnecessary worry. Two days past the time we were to get our scores, I could not wait any longer and walked over to the school and asked Ruth the secretary if the grades had come in.

"Yes, I think Carol tried to call you. Let me check to see if she has gone for the day." Ruth dialed the number as I waited, and when she hung the phone, smiling she assured, "You passed."

I beamed, "Wow! Yummy! You know that means I got all nine problems right," as I clapped my hands and reiterated, "We had ten problems, and we had to make 90 percent!" Ruth was so happy for me. "You did it. Are you going to celebrate?"

"No, I got to go back to work, and I hope I can make it. My knees felt all wobbly." I called Betty, and we shouted "Hallelujah!" together as she had gotten her word the day before. That evening, upon arrival at home, I shared with Ellis and Chucky my success, and all they wanted to know was how much longer did I have to go.

As we took more courses, the number of students continued to drop. Only thirteen of us took the comprehensive exams, which consisted of two eight-hour-day exams that included research, area of focus, and theory. During the exams I wrote so hard I had cramps in my hands. So during the break time as Ken and Ms. Hale snacked, I rubbed and massaged my hands.

We waited a couple of weeks for the results, which determined whether we were eligible to proceed with the remainder of the courses and the dissertation. I did not agonize or worry as much because the exams could be repeated three times if you failed. Thankfully, I passed the first time.

In my last year I was awarded a fellowship from the Achievement Rewards for College Scientist (ARCS) foundation and received a monthly stipend. It came in handy to pay the typist for all of the papers, which ranged from $100 to $150 per paper. Like a scalpel, receiving the fellowship radically lifted the scar tissues from the wound I sustained from being denied scholarships when I was at Alvin. Thanks to many years of good experience at TWU, the Alvin scars were atrophying nicely.

As the remaining semesters ticked on by it became apparent that there was only one person who was nearly ready for graduation. When I realized that person was me, the drive to finish became pressurized. The professors were supportive in reading the chapters of my dissertation and getting them back to me.

Each time they returned them laden with red pencil marks. As I reviewed page after page, it felt like mosquito bites, short-lasting stings that made me cry "Ouch," without becoming paralyzed. There were endless sixty-mile round trips from my home to Rosie Lee, the typist, who lived in Pearland. On many occasions, Ellis made two trips a day taking edited pages back for retyping. Rosie did not have a computer, just a regular typewriter, but was considered the typing czarina for TWU students. Because of her excellent skills and knowledge of APA format (a university requirement for formatting scientific papers), she was in high demand.

Pulling together feedback from four different professors, I felt like Anthony Gatto, the world's greatest juggler. Many times the professors contradicted each other or would have me undo what was approved the last time. Over the months I became skilled in coordinating their suggestions and recommendations. Multiple retyping was necessary. In the midst of this intellectual battle, Rosie Lee, who was overstrapped with typing, asked if I could find someone else to help so I could meet the deadline.

Two steps from going totally hysterical, I phoned Judy, my niece in California, for her friend Betty's phone number. Betty was happy to do it. She was a great typist but did not know APA format. Rosie Lee agreed to work with her, and within two weeks, she confirmed that Betty was a quick learner and ideal for the job. She was ten miles from my house and had a computer, but many trips had to be made to her office because I did not have a computer or fax machine.

No matter the emotional climate, my role was to keep focused. Betty was kind and did not mind putting in the extra time regardless of the changes. Yet every now and then, I had to sucker punch negative feelings as they seeped into my cerebral cortex. I did not have the time or the energy to waste by developing a counterproductive attitude. This was my dissertation, and I needed all the help and advice I could get.

Luckily for me, my advisors were genuine and interested in me getting it right, so I accepted their peculiarities and for the most part they tolerated mine. At times I had sensory overload. When my stress teetered on the brink of my limits, at that moment I could not go another step. I retreated, walked away from the dissertation, and fought off the temptation to quit as powerful right and left jabs to my head kept sneaking in, bobbing to the right, "Yes, stay" and to the left, "No, quit." After refueling for a few hours or days, head clear, I got back into the ring.

The last two months were filled with chaos and roadblocks. One night around 11:15 p.m., I had to get to Jesse Jones Library, a thirteen-mile trip, before midnight to verify a reference. I made Chuck come with me. We arrived at the library 11:45 p.m., and I made a mad dash for the periodical section. Lo and behold, the journal was nowhere in sight.

I looked and looked, and then the loudspeaker pager informed us that the library would be closing in five minutes. An all-consuming panic began to mount. I hurried to the front desk receptionist and tearfully pleaded, "Please help me find this journal. It's not on the shelf."

Reluctantly, she got up from her seat and retrieved the periodical from the cart where books to be reshelved were held. "Here it is."

I uttered a thank you and literally flew to the Xerox machine on the second floor only to discover it was turned off. All machines were turned off prior to the final closing announcement. I ran back to the first floor to the front desk mumbling, "The machine is off. Please turn it back on. I got to have this reference."

Again, the lady reluctantly came to my rescue and assured, "Okay, I'll turn the Xerox back on."

Tears I had been holding on spewed forth like a fountain.

This time she looked at me with tenderness and asked, "What else can I do for you?"

Consumed by stress and not able to respond, I just shook my head and walked away sobbing. After I completed copying the article, I went to the front desk, composed, and gave her a proper appreciation. "Thank you so much for understanding and for your help."

All the way home I meditated and prayed to maintain my sanity and sustain the drive to finish. I was in the final rounds. I racked up a $3,300 bill for the typing of the dissertation. Surviving the uppercuts, displaced nose, and blows to the chin, I met the deadline. It was a magnificent feat.

I was ready to defend the dissertation before my committee. I took Chuck with me to the meeting. Carol, my chair, encouraged me, "You are prepared," and I believed her! The day of the meeting I took the *Daily Word* with me and sat at the round table, read it, and then laid it where we were to sit. Dr. Rutledge who was not on my committee was the first to come to the table. When she saw my spiritual book, she asked, "Who is the *Daily Word* for? We don't need that." "It's for me, and I need it," I replied with confidence.

When Dr. Wolfe, Dr. Ragsdale, Dr. Vokaty, and Dr. Adamson gathered, the questioning began. At first I could feel my heart thumping in my chest and the air going in and out of my nostrils in a rhythmic flow as I sat poised to take them on. As I presented the research study and findings, my confidence began to rise, my heart and respiratory rates returned to normal. I answered the questions freely, and there were no surprises except Dr. Rutledge asked questions that were not necessarily pertinent to my study. Upon completion, they asked me to step out of the room while a decision was made as to whether I met the requirements.

Chuck and I went outside, and the first thing he said was, "Momma, you kept saying *er* and *er*." I replied, "Oh no, did I?" That made me skeptical. We walked around the campus and chatted until summoned to return to the room.

Carol asked, "How do you think you did?"

"I felt I did well except perhaps said *er* and *er* too many times as identified by Chuck."

They smiled, and Carol said a few words to Chuck and then she and the committee congratulated me on doing a great job. I thanked them for their help and patience.

I walked out into the hallway submerged in a euphoric moment too awesome to describe. The three-year battle had come to an end; it was over, and what a sweet victory. Follow your heart; don't listen to others who can't make sense out of why you are going to school. I thanked God. My mind traveled back to the days when I prayed just to be an RN, and the first thought that came to mind is God's plan is much greater than mine.

I had to come down from the mountain of joy and face the remainder of the process. The last step to closing out the requirements for graduation was to be sure every word on each sheet of the 192-page dissertation fell within the template in order to be approved. To do that I had to place each sheet of the dissertation on to this template, hold it up to light to determine whether all letters fell inside the margin. They all were right.

After much hectic activity and excitement, I was able to get all of the papers and the dissertation ready, but I had only one-day turnaround time to get it to the main campus in Denton. My options were to send it by one of the professors who was going to the Denton campus or to fly it in myself. So Ellis took the plane into Dallas, rented a car, and drove into Denton to deliver it.

The day of the flight I was home meditating and reflecting on the climax of the three-year matriculation when suddenly a newsbreak flashed across the television screen. They announced that a plane to Dallas had caught fire. I gasped and cried, "Oh my God," thinking my dissertation had burned up and did not get to Denton on time. There was no cell phone or beeper to call Ellis. As visions of fire, smoke, and flames raced across my mind, I rationalized that nothing had happened to Ellis because the airline stewards probably got all of the passengers off the plane. Having to hurry, the five by eight box with the three copies of my 192-page dissertation most likely had to be left on the plane.

This was an emergency. No time should be wasted on that box. While it was my career-life package, its value did not equate with Ellis's life. If there was something he could do, I know he would do his best. My nursing and spiritual values started to kick in, so I walked, fretted, took in deep breaths, and prayed for hours.

When I did not hear from him, I resigned that the dissertation was now in ashes. Gripped by fear, I was drained and felt hopeless. I did not think to call the airlines.

Then around 10:00 p.m. Ellis called to say he met with Dean Gudmundsen and personally gave her the dissertation. He was going to spend the night in Dallas with friends and take the early flight home the next day. Aware that a plane had caught fire but it was not the one he was on, he saw no need to call. I was relieved, thankful, and angry at the same time that he waited so long to call, but instead of saying anything negative, I squeezed the phone and held my tongue.

Feeling relieved, suddenly a glint of panic muscled its way into my few minutes of peace. I remembered Carol explaining to me that technically I was finished, but the dean could read the dissertation and find something to change.

When Carol finally reassured me everything was complete and in good shape, I couldn't believe it. I had to reconcile with myself that the battle was over, and the verdict had been announced. My husband would soon be married to a doctor, and Chuck would have a momma doctor. Without their support, this would not have happened.

As I prepared for graduation, which was later in the same month, I became cool as a cucumber; the worrying and frustration was over. I stayed the course. I had given it my best and had a lot of support. Now it was time I claim the blessing that everything was all right. I could now raise my hand and declare myself as the super middle weight champion.

It was quite cold the day of graduation as Ellis, Chucky, Iris, Edward, Sylvia, and Isaac witnessed me being hooded as the lone graduate from the Houston campus doctoral program. Not only was it a historical event for me and my family but also for Texas Woman's University at the Houston campus. Their first doctoral program successfully had a graduate who just happened to be me.

Feelings of warmth, thanksgiving, and joy filled my heart as I reflected on the path that I had traveled. I knew Momma was saying from up above, "You are blessed." Daddy was crowing, "Gal, I told ya, ya waz apt." I did not feel pious or haughty; there was a sense of pride deep in my spirit. It is amazing what you can do when you persevere. The ability to triumph begins with you. To accomplish great things, you can dream about them, but you must act. You have to get up off that ever-loving canvas.

When I announced at work that I had received my doctorate and was now Dr. Mary Holt Ashley, the queries as to whether I were to be called doctor began. I gave them a choice of calling me Ashley or Dr. Ashley but no longer Mrs. Ashley. The first time I was paged as Dr. Ashley the operators wanted to know if I was working in physician services. I did a lot of explaining to all levels of employees that nurses who earn doctorates are doctors also. After a few months it settled in, and everyone seemed okay with the title. For many years, there was no other nurse at our hospital with that auspicious title.

Dr. Sears invited me to his staff meeting and presented me with flowers and a plaque for earning my doctorate. Dr. Eknoyan had the diploma permanently sealed as a gift to me, and the staff gave me a nice reception. They put together their money to make it happen because there was no such fund available to support that kind of recognition. The *Houston Chronicle* newspaper ran a story about my success, and there were other recognitions that were carried out in my honor by nursing organizations and friends.

Several months later, knee-deep into work, employees commenced to question whether I was going to stay at Ben Taub or go somewhere else since I had a doctorate. I made myself clear that I was working where I wanted to be and had no aspirations to go anywhere else.

Later that year, Nancy, a good friend who was the director of education, died from complications of a liver transplant; subsequently her position became available. I applied for it, not because it was my goal but an opportunity to try something different. I was not interviewed. Ruth who was a long-term employee in that department was appointed. I thought, *No problem. She had the experience.* There were no other opportunities for in-house promotion at that time.

I became president of my neighborhood civic club and that was an interesting two years. Getting with the neighbors to achieve community goals was an enriching experience that very much resembled work. As with any group, only a few do the work, and others chime in when there is a specific interest. We worked to establish rules for a safe community, placed deed restrictions, and held lively social gatherings.

On the job we began working on building two new hospitals—one for Jefferson Davis and one for Ben Taub. That was indeed a new level of involvement and a real knowledge broker that gave me that extra boost that jobs need to provide when you have been around a long time. Meetings with architects, planners, and consultants were frequent and time consuming, but I stockpiled new skills.

I loved the learning and contribution I was allowed to make. The sixty-bed wards would become smaller units of thirty-one beds with four four-bed units and seven single rooms. The real excitement was that it was going to make a difference in the patient environment.

Nursing fought for space for nurses' lounges while many of the physician chiefs felt nurses did not need that kind of space. Agreements would be made on certain features, spaces, and locations, but when we reconvened for the next meeting, the architects had met with the physicians and given them more space and deleted or reduced what had been promised for nursing. More political and negotiating techniques came to the surface. Months into the project, balancing the new tasks and carrying out my regular work did not give me the same adrenalin rush I felt when I was in school and working at the same time.

There was a void, so I ran for president of Texas Nurses Association district 9. I won and was then in my element. New horizons always stirred up extra creative juices. The opportunity to lead a professional nursing organization unleashed excitement and new, untapped skills. Volunteer help was managed and facilitated differently from paid staff where you have a defined line of authority. My skills to influence people were heightened through this type of leadership experience as I adapted to the role.

Over the next few years, we prepared for a metamorphosis and were ready to move January 1990 into the new hospital. The units were prepped, and the staff successfully moved all patients. A new way of operating began. The updated new furniture, nice painted walls, open nursing stations, enclosed patient rooms, and other amenities added flair to the hospital environment and generated pride among staff and administration. Patients and their families were also pleased. Head nurses for the first time had their own offices located in close proximity to their unit.

To my surprise, the biggest complaint came from patient caregivers who were accustomed to wards where they observed their patients in a wide sweep without having to do as much walking. They bitterly complained about the amount of walking necessitated to go in and out of patient rooms. The new patient call system gave patients quick access to the staff, thus patient requests increased.

There were several meetings concerning issues related to the perceived increase in workload. We hooked on to the Work Smart Not Harder motto and made some adjustments. Change, even when it is good, does not always bring out the best in people immediately, but overtime, adaptation occurs. Leaders are change agents who accelerate and decelerate movements to ensure outcomes.

As nursing continued to change and grow, head nurse titles were changed to nurse managers. They assumed more administrative accountability for their units such as budgeting, hiring, goal setting, and whatever other details had to be attended to. They were given additional training, and there was a new level of expectation. The inception of new duties such as budgeting, productivity measurements, and required computer skills exposed different levels of weaknesses among the managers. Even with group and individual training, for some, adaption was minimal. Managers began to spend more time in their office doing "paperwork" as they described it and less time in the clinical area. Staff and physicians complained about their lack of accessibility and availability.

Frustrations and lack of confidence saturated the managers' spirit, causing morale to plummet to an all-time low. They were not able to achieve a balance in their work distribution. As I examined the situation, several issues were considered: reeducation, individual support, assignment of another nurse manager as a buddy, and group discussions among the team. I employed these variables to assist the managers to adapt.

Each began to adjust, however, I recognized that everyone was at a different skill level. My best option was to capitalize on their strengths, which in turn boosted their level of confidence. Two years working within this framework, we were again a strong team.

Each director was allotted a full-time personal secretary with office space, so I hired Vanessa. I experienced what it felt like to have three hands. She was a speedball and could keep up with me and was devoted to the medicine department. My work output tripled because I no longer had to impose upon the secretary who was overloaded with work from two directors. Even my creativity rose to another level because I could draft a proposal and have it typed over and over again until it met my satisfaction without settling for less because my work was not the only request for a particular secretary.

Great leadership is contingent upon a continuous renewal process, grounded in experiencing the new through studying, networking, and applying new ways of doing and being. My best is actualized when I am challenged above the status quo or expectation. I reveled in the effort to try something new even at the risk of being turned down. There is risk in not taking risk.

I developed the first preceptor program for my staff after reading how it helped new nurses to adapt to their environment when they had one person throughout their orientation. Making the right connection to the work environment during the first weeks of employment has positive retention benefits.

At the end of the preceptor rotation, a luncheon was held to reward the preceptors for a job well done although administration declined to fund it. The nurse managers and I sponsored it from our personal resources. It was worth all of the efforts when the preceptors walked into the room for the event. Their appreciation was my reward.

The education department was interested in the concept; hence, Derotha decided it was a great idea, so it became a district model that was refined over and over again throughout the years and is still in existence.

As the president of TNA, I had an idea of developing a recognition program for nurses, so I visited P. K. in Louisiana who was a gracious and charming host. She provided me a memorable stay at one of the finest hotels. I attended her great one hundred-nurse recognition program where one hundred nurses including RNs and LVNs were recognized for their achievement at an informal event. It was a beautiful affair, and I loved the concept; however I dreamed of a recognition program that was more formal.

I presented the idea to the TNA board, and they liked it. Lynn was especially supportive and excited about the idea. We decided to recognize only twenty nurses and to have them meet criteria related to professional practice, role model quality, and commitment to the profession. Nurses were nominated by their peers, superiors, or patients. A panel of reviewers scored the applications, and the twenty nurses with the highest score became the outstanding nurses for that year. They were given a plaque and recognized at a banquet titled Nursing Celebration. The inception of the program in 1991 was coincidently the same night that basketball great Magic Johnson announced he had contracted HIV. The recognition program has remained a stellar annual event for nurses in Houston. I have only missed attending one time.

In 1992, Shirley, a friend and TNA coworker, asked if she could nominate me as one of the ten Women on the Move that was sponsored by the *Houston Post* newspaper and the Texas Executive Women. I was honored that she considered me worthy of such a prestigious award. She submitted the nomination, and I underwent a lengthy interview process by several prominent women on the panel. After the interview, I said to myself, *Whether I get chosen or not, the interview process boosted my impromptu speaking skills.*

I had read the accomplishments of nominees in the past years and was amazed at their contributions. Waiting for the results was not marked with anxiety or doubts but with an attitude that it would be an indicator of how my career journey was measured against others. The wait was more like waiting for my grade to be posted because I felt good about the exam; thus I expected an A.

On a Sunday afternoon, arriving from church as usual, I hurried into the kitchen to warm up the food that I had cooked on that Saturday night. As I started toward the kitchen, the phone rang, and a tiny wave of resentment crept into my spirit as I said, "I am hungry, and I don't have time to talk to nobody." My conscience however, said, *I can't ignore the phone no matter how hungry I am.*

I answered it. An unfamiliar voice, "May I speak to Dr. Ashley?"

Immediately, I knew it had to be work or community-related because no one addressed me with that title outside of work. The voice continued with, "This is Texas Executive Women for Women on the Move."

I stopped and dropped down in the nearest chair to receive the news.

The voice said, "I am calling to congratulate you on being selected as one of the ten Women on the Move."

"Thank you! Oh my God, thank you!" I said as I listened for further instructions while stomping my feet and moving my head up and down in joyous celebration.

I hung up the phone, leapt toward the kitchen, cut the fires off from under the pots, and walked back into the den without my plate.

Ellis asked, "You not eating?"

"I can't. Do you know who that was on the phone?" I asked in a voice trembling with excitement.

Startled, he took his eyes off the football game long enough to ask, "What? What happened?"

"I was selected as one of the ten Women on the Move." A man who rarely gives accolades or commendations, Ellis shot me a side grin, which implied he was proud.

The recognition event was a gala affair with more than 800 people in attendance. Family, friends, and coworkers accompanied me to the affair. Each of the ten women's career highlights was emphasized as she walked across the stage during a spectacular ceremony. The *Houston Post* newspaper pictured each recipient in color along with a career bio in the social section of the newspaper. I have kept in contact with a couple of the ladies who received the honor at the same time, and I attend the annual reunion reception as often as time permits.

This achievement was a phenomenal moment in my career in that my contributions as a leader were recognized and aligned with women who were bank executives, lawyers, physicians, administrators, entrepreneurs, and community leaders. I began to sense that everything I was putting into my career matters; there is no wasted or meaningless time, and the joy that manifests itself on the inside of me is being transformed in my work and acts to gain respect from others. The joy of work gave me a relentless drive to grow, change, and improve nursing environments for the sake and benefit of patients, employees, and the organization.

My passion to work exceeded my need for money or status, giving me energy to persevere toward higher goals. Each day I awaken I was excited about going to work, knowing there would be more than enough chaos and turbulence to challenge my critical thinking skills. The opportunity to figure out how to gain leverage and stay afloat was a dangling carrot before my eyes.

I learned to appreciate life's hard lessons and the beauty of perseverance, so I stayed poised for championship matches.

The battles included a myriad of events, tasks, goals, and expectations that required physical, emotional, intellectual, and spiritual energy in order to achieve results. At the same time, I refueled my own passion and drive as I looked for ways to influence, negotiate, and create in order to maintain an environment for employees to deliver excellent outcomes. There is much joy in doing work that benefits the staff, and it trickles down to the patients and to the organization.

The empowerment value of joy intrigued me to the point that I developed a lecture entitled "Experiencing Joy in the Workplace" that I have presented many times over the years. I discovered from talking to participants at workshops and seminars that a high rate of people in nursing, whether at the staff, manager, or leader levels felt joyless in their work environment.

I personally believe joy is an entitlement in the workplace. Why spend ten to twelve hours a day doing something that does not bring a certain amount of joy? As diverse as the job market is, there is opportunity for you to find that job in which you can experience joy in your work; if not, I encourage you to leave it. In addition, the organization is obligated to ensure that the work environment has the elements that promote and inspire you to have a joyful experience.

Experiencing joy does not mean there are no rocky times; that's part of the equation. My battles were too numerous to count. A constant battle existed between emergency services and medicine in the admission of patients due to no vacancies or slow bed turnover. Looking for beds was exhaustive and stress producing. Everyone was involved: staff, physicians, administration, and all departments, as we struggled to discharge and transfer patients.

It seemed as if there was no end. Staff understood that those found to have held beds without releasing them were subject to reprimand. Every conceivable strategy was attempted to free up beds sooner. I developed a discharge holding area where patients who were discharged but delayed from exiting the bed were housed until they left the hospital.

For patients to be eligible they had to be in a self care state. They were placed in comfort chairs with access to a television in a room designated as the discharge holding. Patients were observed and provided with food until discharge. The use of the discharge holding area increased bed availability. After a year of utilizing it, the processes were refined, and I later published the results in the *Journal of Nursing Administration*. It is still in existence.

A seeker of new challenges, after serving my term as president of TNA district 9, I worked on the finance and nomination committees at the state level then ran for vice president. My campaign took off with a theme "Vote for Mary Holt Ashley: The nurse to lead Texas into the future for change."

Having never campaigned for an office before, I gained some pointers and support from Ana, a friend and experienced board member. She had lots of connections throughout the state and was a good mentor. It was a great challenge, a network expansion of friends and additional skills. I won the election and was the first black nurse to hold an office at the state level. It was a two-year commitment.

Surprised and quite pleased, I gained administrative support from Mrs. Frazier to attend the quarterly two-day board meetings in Austin using hospital business days. For the first time I did not have to use my vacation days to attend professional meetings. Her change of heart indicated that she now felt comfortable in getting the administrator to approve. Thankfully, I did not let past denials preclude me from asking again. This time I got what I requested, thinking to myself, *Harboring a defeatist attitude would have kept me from getting the support I needed.* All leaders change and grow.

Serving in this capacity strengthened my commitment to nursing and enriched my career. The recognized value to my organization having its nurse leader hold a position in a professional organization at the state level increased the organization's visibility and role modeled professional behaviors for its nurses.

No matter how exciting work was for me, there were times I pondered: *Where am I going? Would I remain a middleweight champion [director] my entire career? Should my love for Ben Taub hold me hostage, or should I change jobs? Am I marketable for a vice president's job?*

As I wrestled with these thoughts, they loomed larger than my mind could deal with. No mentor or confidant, I needed to create my own trigger for change, so I decided, "I am going to test the market. I will go on interviews to see what happens." I sought the advice of a headhunter to review my options for a vice president (VP) of nursing, the top position in a health care organization.

The first consultant sent me on two interviews, and the second one I followed through to the job offer phase and politely turned it down because Chuck did not want me to work out of town and come home on the weekends. He was a junior in high school and wanted me available at home to help with different projects. I conceded his request because he was supportive to me throughout my educational pursuits. It felt good to know I was marketable.

Two years later, still hankering for a promotion, I hired another consultant to find a VP position in Houston. Terry assessed my resume, "You've been in the district too long, and right now, Mary, to be honest with you, what I can do for you would be to get you a lateral position because VP positions for blacks are almost nonexistent in this part of the country. A private facility may not value your leadership experience from the county hospital."

Stunned by her assessment and fraught with emotions, I decelerated the thoughts that flew into my mind. No hard feelings for Terry. I ended the meeting with, "Well, I guess that is the reality I must face. At least I know."

That same day, just as I got home I received a frantic call from my sister Louise. "Mae, I just got a call from Shawn saying Kim just shot at him."

"What? Is she all right?"

"I don't know. I'm on my way over there, and I need you to come with me. I know where he lives, but I don't know the name of the street. I am so scared and too nervous to think, but when I get there, I will call you and give you the address."

Consumed by a pulse-pounding reaction, I struggled with fear as I waited and reminisced. Kim, my beautiful niece, a senior nursing student at Prairie View College of Nursing, was having problems with her boyfriend. She and I had several long conversations, and she had resolved to let him go, but they got back together. The wait for the call seemed an eternity; meanwhile, I called Ana to discuss my interview. Then the call waiting came through. Louise was screaming and hollering, "Kim is dead." I began to scream and scream and dropped the phone.

Chuck bolted out of his room. "Momma, Momma, what is the matter?" I continued screaming for the next few minutes. I could not say it. He kept asking.

Finally, I moaned, "Kim is dead."

Chuck ran from the room. Kim was his favorite cousin. Minutes elapsed before I could put the phone on the hook. When I hung up, it immediately rang. The officer told me to meet Louise at Hermann hospital, and I kept asking what was wrong with her and where was Kim. He replied, "Ma'am, just meet her at the hospital." I pleaded with him to tell me if she really was dead, to no avail. He hung up, and I tried to call somebody but could not think of any phone numbers.

After multiple attempts trying to find someone to take me to the hospital, I lucked out and correctly dialed Eula's number. Her son Bret answered and asked, "What's the matter, Mrs. Ashley?" All I could do was sob. He hung the phone up and beeped his mother and told her I was crying. She was en route home, but instead she came straight to my house. After several minutes of woeful weeping, I conveyed what had happened, and she took me to the hospital.

There we learned the sobering truth that Kim had committed suicide, and Louise was being held in the observation unit for shock. Shawn was not injured. Our entire family was traumatized and shocked. We got through the funeral with support from so many people. March 21, 1994, is imprinted forever in my memory.

The lingering thoughts about the suicide coupled with the bleak forecast about my career mobility cast a dark shadow. It was a double whammy, a scathing technical knockout (TKO). I needed to be carried off the canvas. The pain was deep and unrelieved by my conventional coping strategies. For months and months I tortured myself on each issue as to what should have happened and what was currently happening. The death was beyond my control, but it did not stop me from being angry with God and questioning his relevancy. Momma was not here to reassure me of God's goodness.

I was afraid and remorseful that I felt this way and confessed openly to God for forgiveness. I read the Bible and a lot of self-help books on grief with the most powerful one being *When God Doesn't Make Sense* by Charles Dobson. On the job, I pushed every muscle to its maximum to stay afloat. I began to heal, and within that year, I returned to championship shape.

In 1995 the district offered a severance package to those fifty-five and above to retire. My boss and the hospital administrator took the packet, and the VP position became available. It was an unexpected breakthrough in my career; the potential to be promoted to my dream position existed right in my own place of employment.

Ruth, senior vice president for nursing, called a meeting with all of the nursing directors throughout the district and informed us that the position would be posted. Those interested could apply, and she wanted to know who was interested in the VP position. I was the only one who raised my hand to affirm my interest. Later, others did establish interest.

I assumed there would be an interview process, and a selection would take place. Ruth informed me that the interview process would be conducted differently in that a panel comprised of deans from three local universities along with her, the hospital administrator, and chief of staff would make the selection. That was the first time that method had been employed, and I was curious as to why it was used. I did not ask Ruth, to avoiding putting her on the spot. Based on what I knew and felt about the position, I had my own answer. Nonetheless, my thoughts were, *May the best candidate be chosen.*

Preparation for the interview was much like a boxer preparing for the heavyweight championship; I put in extra work and practiced answering anticipated questions. I was about to enter into the ring where only the champ will remain standing. Reflection on those interviews that I had a year ago enhanced my preparation; otherwise, it would have been over twenty years since I had been interviewed for a job. I believed that "all things work together for the good of those who love the Lord and are called for a purpose."

The day of the interview I did not wear a typical interview navy or black suit. I chose a pale yellowish gold Austin Reed suit, the guru of women's business suits, and simple gold jewelry. A special look for what I hoped to be a significant day in my career. Upon arrival to work, I walked up to the nursing units to make rounds where I talked and greeted employees. Their friendliness and warmth provided a sense of connection and gave me a quick dose of nurturing that boosted my confidence.

They were unaware I was interviewing for my dream job; only the nurse managers knew. Around 10:10 a.m., I was summoned to come to administration. When I entered the waiting area, there sat Carol, my former dissertation chair, dressed in a similar colored suit as I. She was now the dean of TWU Houston campus. What a surprise! Good karma was in the air. I did not expect to see her mainly because I did not know which colleges were selected.

When all arrived, except Dr. Braithwaite, dean of Prairie A&M University, who was ill, the meeting began. Seated at the table were Dr. Stark from University of Texas; Dr. Adamson from Texas Woman's University; Dr. Mattox, chief of staff; Mr. Adams, hospital administrator; and Mrs. Franklin, senior vice president of nursing. The interview went smoothly with Dr. Mattox asking the most questions and giving me relevant situations to solve. I did not feel anxious or tense. Exiting the interview process, I bumped into the next candidate whom I did not know but later found out that all three of us had doctorates and varying degrees of experience.

Nearing my office door, there stood Ann, my secretary, who immediately asked, "Dr. A, how did it go?" I reiterated who the interviewers were and that I felt comfortable in responding to their questions. "We just have to wait and see what happens." I consumed myself with work for the next several hours until I received a call to come to Mrs. Franklin's office. Without emotions or preconceived thoughts, I walked with dignity to her office, knowing that this moment represented a turning point in my career one way or the other. Today I would have an answer.

When I walked into her office, she looked aghast so I quickly said, "Mrs. Franklin, its okay if I wasn't chosen. I'll be okay."

Her eyes brimming with tears enunciated sadness, so I became quiet and waited. Shaking her head she said, "Thank God for the outside people on the panel. You are it."

A quizzical look came across my face, and I felt somewhat threatened by the ambiguity in her body language and her verbal response. I said, "Okay," and constrained myself as I listened to what she had to say.

"This has been tough, but it has worked out. Because of the knowledgeable people on the committee, it worked in your behalf. I am just so glad you got it."

Knowing the professional she was, I accepted her response without further discussion. Years passed before I broached the subject again as to why she was so tearful.

Since Mrs. Franklin lauded the external interviewers, I surmised that all on the panel did not vote for me. Did not the administrator or chief of staff vote for me? For that question, I did not seek confirmation or denial. Never mind, I got the trophy.

Though I faced stiff competition, like Muhammad Ali, I walked away with the heavyweight title. Not with a smirk but sheer joy that I was now credentialed with the title of vice president of nursing. A bird does not sing because it has an answer; it sings because it has a song. I was ready and excited to do the job.

Leadership Point

Round Eight

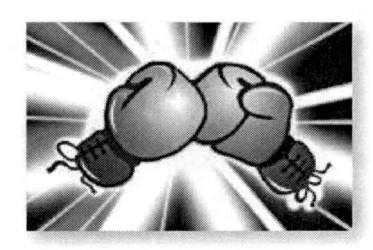

Produce outcomes that belong in the Hall of Fame

1. Aim to win and achieve honestly.
2. Seek excellence and your work will speak for you.
3. Believe that extraordinary strategies yield extraordinary outcomes that bring organizational success, honor and recognition.
4. Celebrate your team because leadership victories are team driven.
5. Challenge your team to the next victory.

CHAPTER 9

Light Heavyweight Champion

THE FIRST MAJOR change in my new role was to consolidate the three nursing services: emergency and ambulatory service, operative service, and inpatient service, deleting two of the vice president positions and placing all of nursing under my span of control. This was a major change for the entire hospital—more like trying to unite three hospitals rather than nursing services. The prediction was that there would be an uproar and major resistance. Rumor had it that the emergency and ambulatory service were going to boycott the change.

Armed with my practical philosophy that leaders are obligated to influence staff to work together toward a common goal, I set up the first meeting. Everyone showed up, and each director was asked to give ideas and commit to uniting into one team. Many meetings took place.

Three departments were without directors: medicine, my former department; women and infant service; and emergency and ambulatory. In addition, there were several clinics within the ambulatory service without nurse managers. I devised a temporary reporting schedule and met with the physicians of each department to apprise them of the situation and ask for their support. Because I knew the least about women and infants service, I donned my scrubs for a week and followed nurses around to get the hang of clinical operations. Having never seen a baby born, I hoped to get the chance, but it did not happen. Unfortunately, I finished my career without ever witnessing a live birth.

I met separately with the chief physician of ambulatory and the chief of women services every two weeks until a director was hired for each department. Using an interview process comprised of the physicians from the service, chief of staff, and me, candidates were selected within three months.

Chaos and confusion, while not overtaxing, existed as adaptation took place for me and my newly acquired employees. The consolidation of policies and procedures to the extent possible and appropriate was an ongoing process for the next three years. The most remarkable and encouraging outcome in the first year was that there were no major wars between the inpatient and outpatient staff. The scramble to acquire beds that always led to finger-pointing and overexaggeration still existed but was now viewed more objectively, leading to manageable resolutions.

The major and most traumatic change occurred in the emergency psychiatric area. There were insurmountable patient care and management issues that could not be corrected without clearing out the existing management team, nurse manager, and three assistant nurse managers. It took almost four months to resolve it and maintain a degree of confidentiality until each manager had been informed and placed in staff nurse positions.

During the process, I had a flashback to 1988 when my favorite coach, Tom Landry of the Dallas Cowboys, was fired by the owner Jerry Jones through the media. Coach Landry was the last to know. That process was reprehensible to me; hence I dropped football from my list of pastimes. The images from that fiasco helped me to focus on carrying out terminations and demotions using the most meticulous process. At best, it is filled with hurt feelings and damaged relationships with the persons involved and the remaining staff.

After successful reorganization of the nursing services and the emergency psychiatric department, things rolled into the normal routine as I continued to build a cohesive team. Mandatory meetings included a biweekly directors meeting and a monthly leadership meeting for all leaders and managers. At first some of management was resistant to these meetings, but in time adjustments were made, and they notified Carla if they were going to be absent. Diane said to me, "Shucks, Dr. Ashley, we are not used to all these formal meetings, and we got to train ourselves." I smiled and quipped, "Okay." It is refreshing when an employee tells you just "how the cow eats the cabbage."

In January of each year, we had a state of the union meeting for nursing where each department showcased its significant outcomes, and I presented the overall nursing goals and outcomes. Each department put their best PowerPoint presentation forward. Chief physicians and administrators were invited to attend. Structured communications among departments helped to develop unity and share best practices.

Over the years there were some directors who voiced that the state of the union had become too competitive. I reiterated repeatedly that this was to be their proudest moment of the year, and however each of them presented it was their choice. The "too competitive" statement bugged me, so I inquired of the group of directors if we should continue to have it. There was a resounding yes vote.

From the discussion, I discerned that the main peeve was the difference in the quality of the PowerPoint presentation due to the skill level of the secretary. The presentations were not required to be PowerPoint, but it appeared to be the method of choice. I solicited Carla, who had expert skills in that area and was a master teacher, to find a way to work with the secretaries on developing PowerPoints. She helped them, and they were ready by the end of the year. The returned excitement was exhibited at the next annual meeting.

A simple act I started that became my branded signature throughout my career was to add to each letter, e-mail, or note, "Thanks for being on my team." I popped the cap on my thirty-five-year bottle and let out the memories of those feelings of appreciation I experienced while working at the cab stand when Mr. Conley said thank you. I used this statement for the remaining years of my career, and if I forgot it, which was rare, the employee would ask, "Am I still on your team? You did not say it in the e-mail you sent." It proved to be one my highest payoffs. At my retirement party, the worth of that statement was referred to several times.

Working as the vice president of nursing with responsibility for all areas of nursing, I made a concerted effort to get to know the people throughout the hospital just as I knew the medicine department. Meetings, rounds, small groups, and one-on-one interactions helped me to develop relationships throughout the hospital while keeping a balance. Since I had had a long-standing relationship with the medicine department, employees observed to see if I relinquished that protective relationship to one that was encompassing and inclusive of the additional departments as well.

The success indicator was that there were no human resource grievances or personal complaints levied against me; thus it was safe to say I made the transition. Prior to my leadership of the emergency department, they were notorious for calling in the news media when they felt problems were not resolved to their satisfaction. As we continued to develop an inclusive culture for nursing, changes were instituted that produced phenomenal growth in that area, and problem solving was relegated to an internal process.

The noticeable difference in the vice president and director roles was the increased span of control while at the same time having the same number of hours in a day. I had to filter out some of my strategies for maintaining interpersonal relationships that did not work for larger groups. Never losing sight that employees are my greatest resource, maintaining relationships was still a high priority. The accountabilities were significantly greater, but that is where the real learning takes place. Leadership is as much about becoming as it is doing.

The district quality department reported quarterly the number of patient complaints that every department within each hospital received. Of course, nursing, who has the most contact with patients, usually had the highest number of complaints. Each time that report circulated at the quality meetings when Ben Taub's numbers came up, if they were high, I wanted the floor to open up and swallow me. I was not ashamed of nursing but was distressed that we had not been able to get our arms around this issue.

My natural defense for disappointment is to immediately find a cure or a treatment. I took these reports to the directors, and we strategized ways to reduce complaints, taking into consideration that change starts in the parking lot and not just at the bedside. A patient or family who encounters a problem prior to being admitted to a particular unit may sustain the hurt and disappointment throughout the admission. Then they are dissatisfied with nursing care as well as the service.

We were not defensive; we were just trying to devise the best offense strategy as we reviewed complaints and talked one-on-one with patients and families. We knew that the work that needed to be done was far-reaching throughout the district.

I noticed repeatedly at each of my leadership meetings that the discussion of patient complaints left the directors and nurse managers feeling saddened and low in spirit. Unless that sense of doom was abated, it would be difficult to motivate the leaders who in turn needed to get their staff on board to work on this important issue. Providing emotional leadership for my leaders would be difficult if I myself did not maintain a positive attitude.

I pumped myself up by reflecting on my dad's attitude when Christmas rolled around, and there were no toys or gifts. He took charge in his own way of getting us in a good mood, using a variety of humor and storytelling. He did not let circumstances get in the way. There was a sense of urgency, and I too must do something. Guided by the principle of leaving no stone unturned, I brainstormed on strategies.

I attempted to get the quality department to look proportionally at the number of unsolicited thank-you letters that I received concerning the care staff rendered to patients, not with the intention of negating the complaints, but giving an overall picture of how the units were perceived. It was not considered. I created the Patient Choice Award where the letters that I received each month from patients and families were read by a panel of employees. The employee or unit that received the most compassionate letter was invited to attend the leadership meeting and was given the award.

It motivated staff on each unit to do exceptionally nice things for the patients. There were further efforts to reduce patient complaints: two RN positions were converted into four customer service advocates—the first for the district. Their roles were to anticipate and meet patient needs to reduce patient complaints, which gained respect, and their contribution readily became noticeable. Eventually, they were transferred from my span of control to become a district service that was expanded to both hospitals, and the numbers increased.

To get every unit and department involved in a project, I challenged them to take their thank-you and commendation letters and make quilts. They were to be hung throughout the hospital. Initially most of them saw little value in doing this project since a negative impression of their unit existed.

This was a teaching moment right before my eyes in that their nonchalant attitudes could be a hindrance. Attitude determines your altitude. Embracing this concept would be an opportunity to tell their story. Points I iterated in the team-building meeting were the following: (1) the project is a great way for others to know what is going on in your department and unit, (2) it unifies staff toward a common goal, and (3) you will discover some of your employees' best creative skills.

After that team-building session, the directors had a change in attitude and got some of their units to participate. Once a few of the units started working on quilts, creativity, uniqueness, and competition rose to an unbelievable level of excitement. It felt like what Malcolm Gladwell describes in his book *The Tipping Point*. A dramatic change, epidemic in character, started by a few units, infected the others, and fairly soon more joined until all departments had a quilt. Some had several because each unit wanted its own.

When all the quilts were completed, they far exceeded my expectations. They were beautiful, and there was a high level of artistic detail. The morale was high, and it was the talk of the department. We had a quilt viewing, inviting board members, administration, employees, and external guests. It was a spectacular event.

The morning of the showing, at exactly 8:00 a.m., the first person to arrive was Mr. Finder, then chairman of the board of managers. I watched as he visited each quilt and took notes. He was complimentary and expressed commendation to staff.

People internally and externally marveled at the quilts and especially the compassionate manner in which patients and families expressed their appreciation for the care and services they received. The quilts hung for more than six months, and I wrote an article entitled "Patchwork of Excellence" that was published in *Nursing Management*.

The staff, intoxicated with joy from the accolades received, was gently urged to forge ahead and make customer service a high priority. After celebrations were over, it took effort to refocus the team to the job routines. Within a few days, they settled down as high emotions subsided.

Continuing to learn and grow over the last five years, I had many speaking engagements and was comfortable speaking at seminars and nursing pinning ceremonies. I was invited to speak at the Houston Community College nursing ceremony, and with it came an unexpected encounter. The night of the event, when I completed my speech and received adulations, another instructor from the back of the stage came up to talk to me.

As she was coming toward me, she said, "Mary Edna, oh, I am so proud of you, and that speech was so good." I recognized the voice somewhat, and I knew it had to be someone from way back, because I had not used Edna in my name in over twenty years.

It was Mrs. Dupree, one of my instructors from Alvin Junior college. We squeezed and held each other's hands and agreed to talk when the program was over. Immediately after the program, she and I embraced again and talked for a while. She grew solemn. "I wish the nursing director at Alvin could see you." I smiled and offered get well wishes when she said the director was not doing well. Mrs. Dupree promised to visit me at Ben Taub, and we departed. She did visit, and we had a great time.

LEADERSHIP POINT

Round Nine

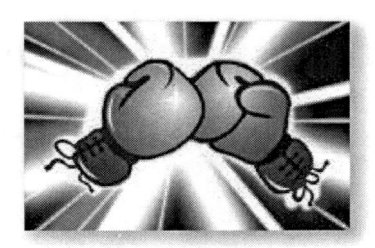

Become a Champion Regardless of your Rank

1. Focus on your knockout punches.
2. Forget whether you are a feather, middle or heavy weight and strive to be the best.
3. Keep in mind, giving your best makes you a champion.
4. Believe championship is a state of mind.
5. Have a passion for what you do.

CHAPTER 10

Middle Heavyweight Champion

ON A DAY when everything was going right, Ann, my secretary, approached me with a surprise. She informed me that she was interested in applying for a job in the district board office. That job was a pay grade higher than what I was paying, and it would be a promotion. I explained to her that I fully support anyone interested in upward mobility; it was no different for her. "If you get the job, it would be a tremendous loss to me, however, I am excited about the possibility for you."

Since I traveled to the administration building one to two times a day, I offered to carry her application over to human resources. She was dumbfounded that I would do that. As we waited with hope for nearly three months, I encouraged her, and we discussed how the work could be accomplished should she get the job. I reminded her that Pam, the special projects coordinator, was an excellent typist and highly skilled in administrative tasks.

Ann did get the job, and several months later, I hired another secretary. Her resume was replete with a high level of experience, and she interviewed well. Within a few weeks, however, there was a noticeable discrepancy between her resume and performance. I attempted to give her a chance as we were in the midst of some heavy-duty projects.

I developed a special project that helped leaders and managers focus on creating an environment that replicated the qualities of a sanctuary based on Lance Secretan's book *Reclaiming Higher Ground: Creating Organizations That Inspire the Soul*. The entire district leadership was excited as we began having meetings to carve out the steps to having a soulful organization. We were on the move.

This project was submitted to the American Organization of Nurse Executives where I received national recognition along with the Organization-Wide Innovation award. Under the new administration, though, this project fell through the cracks.

The entire district underwent change. Mrs. Moore, the chief executive officer (CEO) and long-time employee of the district, retired. Mr. Adams, the deputy administrator, became the interim CEO until the board of trustees hired Mr. Guest. Mr. Adams came to Ben Taub as the administrator. Mr. Lopez was hired as the district's chief operating officer (COO).

My office also was not going in the direction that I had been accustomed to and required. Nine months into the job, the secretary had shown no improvements. She simply could not keep up; consequently, I terminated her.

After several interviews, I hired Carla, a young, multitalented, highly skilled lady with creativity extraordinaire. Working on new ideas and projects excited her, and we worked like Trojans who were thirsty for victory. She was a blessing to me and my directors.

Mr. Adams, hospital administrator, retired, and Mr. Stein became the acting administrator, and we kept the hospital going. After several months, Mr. Cunningham was hired as the administrator. Retired from the air force, he came with a military persona and with a sullen attitude toward me. The first six months, only approaching me when it was absolutely necessary, most of his communication to me was via Mr. Stein who was now the assistant administrator. It puzzled me that he avoided me. Accustomed to such behavior I elected not to push and stayed out of his sight.

Any assignment he gave me via Carla or his secretary I got it done and on time. There were many instances he asked for it early with a hint of impatience. Carla, Pam, and I soon figured out to prepare and have ready any assignment early in anticipation, irrespective of the agreed-upon deadline.

How you cope with difficult situations demonstrates to your peers, employees, and superiors the nature of your character. Your own personal attitude has a lot to do with how you lead and can affect your ability to influence your followers. The directors' support kept me grounded because when your direct reports respect you, they work with and for you to ensure goals are achieved against odds.

George, as he insisted on being called, a retired army colonel, was hired as the associate administrator. He brought a high level of skill and a fresh, friendly spirit to administration that was felt by all. There now existed an administrative team heavily weighted with military men who were as different as night and day. This was the first time in my career where my boss and peers were all men. I now faced a different opponent, had to master military jargon as well as become decisive in the punches to be delivered. I welcomed the challenge.

My title was changed from vice president of nursing to associate administrator for nursing. With the change in title I did not assume any additional assignments; however, it changed my rank and strengthened my role. I moved to middle heavyweight rank. There was a huge difference in the magnitude of challenges that were intensified by the weight of a new personality.

With the new district senior administration intact, a series of other changes took place. The senior vice president for nursing position was deleted, and other district director titles were changed. I reported directly to the hospital administrator instead of dual reporting to the senior vice president of nursing and the hospital administrator.

Experience taught me the difference between power and authority and which of the two gets the best results. When you use power, it generally means you try to force someone to do your will. On the other hand, if you use the authority of your position to get people to willingly do your will, it is a win-win situation for you and the employee. My personal conviction of this principle helped me to succeed in getting employees to be on my team with the sole purpose to make Ben Taub great.

The directors were gung ho in wanting to keep Ben Taub mainstream. My vision for a department of nursing research was again stunted after my research position was not approved for the third year in a row. My mind traveled to a battle where the boxer had lost two or three rounds in a row during the match. The ringside judges scored him low and made predictions that the boxer was loosing. They used such statements as "he is losing;" "he is not landing any effective punches;" or "he is enduring too many heavy blows." When the boxer returned to his corner, the trainer screamed "man, keep your chin up;" "use more jabs to the opponent's weak side:" and "stay off the ropes."

When the bell rung for the start of the next round the trainer hollered; "you go out there and get him." The boxer went to the center of the ring and suddenly threw an uppercut to the opponent's chin that knocked him off center. He followed up with a combination of right and left hooks that staggered the opponent and immediately the judges changed the direction of their comments about the boxer and said "he is coming back, he his recovering."

The boxer's momentum shifted to another level and one perfectly landed hook to the opponent's right jaw knocked him to the canvas. The opponent failed to get up at the count of ten. Quitting when over taken by temporary defeat in the early rounds would have caused the boxer to lose to his opponent. The boxer kept on going.

Reflection on that match uplifted my spirits to a point that I recovered my confidence. I teamed up with the directors who agreed to stretch themselves help me make nursing research a part of the nursing department. Those with master's degrees and some research experience became part of the team. I solicited Dr. Travis, associate dean at TWU Houston Campus, to provide a professor pro bono to teach a six-week research refresher course for the directors. Dr. Kernicki accepted the assignment to teach the course at Ben Taub for two hours twice a week for six weeks. Her research and teaching expertise made it a success. All of the directors, including myself, completed the course.

The research team was ready to go, and within the next two years, they produced a research study to determine the highest call-in rates per classification of workers, prevalent day of the week, shift, and which units. They simultaneously performed their regular duties while working on the research team with me as chair. Upon completion they proudly presented the study results to the staff and administration. A team comprised of Mary, Sue, Isaac, Jenny, and Dough led by Gayle published an article in the *International Journal of Trauma Nursing* using some of the data from the research.

Their tenacity, work ethic, and commitment to the new nursing research venture, in spite of the additional workload, further substantiated my philosophy. When staff is stretched to do meaningful work and derive satisfaction, they will persevere and achieve. The next year, I upgraded a special projects position to director of nursing research, and there were no objections. My long-awaited vision for a department of nursing research was achieved. I sustained the vision, courage, and patience while strategizing to make it happen.

The old cliché acronym, "**T**ogether **E**veryone **A**chieves **M**ore," was operant by the team, and my appreciation of their work was more than words could express. We were professionally hooked to the same goals, had relationships that allowed us to speak opinions freely, and enjoyed each other's company. Sometimes we encountered stalemates that stung like a bee, and when we worked them out, I, like Muhammad Ali, "floated like a butterfly."

The directors often encouraged me. One day Sue was standing with me in the hall, helping me make sense out of a request that was denied. She turned to me and said, "Doesn't he know by now that when he tells you no that you respond with more energy than ever and get things done? Everybody who knows you knows that." Her statement stirred me up, and I got up off the canvas at the count of one.

Unlike amateur or lesser weight champions, heavyweight champions pick their opponents and are real selective about whom they fight. After the first evaluation, which was very good, I quit fighting with myself on how to grow a boss relationship. In the broad scheme of things, I reconciled with myself that the only person I could change was myself. The intensity of my prayers increased, and I happily kept busy doing exciting and challenging work.

I created a monthly leadership series, and all the nursing leaders were required to attend. The leadership presenters were internal and external speakers. Leaders from other departments were invited, and many attended.

Each nursing director, chief of staff, and all of administration including the administrator were assigned a month to present. Dr. Mattox, an excellent speaker who always agreed to speak to nurses, started the series. Mr. Cunningham came to that presentation as the two of them had a great relationship.

His presentation was due later in the year, and when the time arrived, the room was packed as usual. At the end of his presentation, I commended him personally and publicly for participating in our lecture series. From then on, for every program and event nursing sponsored, Mr. Cunningham was invited for opening or closing remarks.

My primary focus was on nursing and developing nurses so that we had a dynamic environment where patients received excellent care from both physicians and nurses. When the staff was happy, I was happy. Already certified in advance nursing administration, I pushed each director to get a certification so that we could influence the staff to work toward theirs. You get the best out of others when you give your best. Ten pediatric nurses took the pediatric exam at the same time, passed it, and earned their certification.

They helped transcend that goal to other areas, motivating their peers to attain certifications. Not a requirement, but it certainly added credentials to support one's level of expertise. There were many who did not support the theory that all RNs needed a certification. The district paid a bonus for attaining a certification and half of the bonus at each recertification.

The directors and I agreed that we would go all out to achieve Magnet status and thus asked Lyndon Baines Johnson (LBJ), our sister hospital, to participate. At first, they declined then later joined the journey to Magnet status. It became an ongoing joint process.

Each of my departments was introduced to branding as a mark of nursing excellence for nursing care. Each developed its own brand. The brands were based on what they wanted patients, families, staff, and others to remember about their units. It appealed to everyone. Within six months each unit had a brand, and for the hospital, "Taub Notch Care" was the brand suggestion submitted by Seidra. Every department got involved, and it became a hospital—and districtwide goal. LBJ's brand was "presidential care." Later the clinics adopted "caring for one patient at a time."

To share the Taub Notch Care brand, we invited the Taub family, for which the hospital was named, to the ceremony, as suggested by Dr. Mattox. We unveiled the brand to the family and the public. Mr. Cunningham was supportive. Thanks to the hard work of Carla, Pam, and Jimmie, the conference room was transformed into an eloquent setting coupled with a sophisticated program that emphasized our new brand "Taub Notch" care and service.

Challenges were motivating for me, and I have a tendency to think that you have to set the bar high in order to achieve the most. Staffing ratios have been problematic nationwide and have been worked on and established by professional standards as a guiding point and some as a required minimum standard. I had toiled with a new and exciting, in my opinion, strategy that would motivate staff to accomplish their work in a "step out of the box" manner.

Traditionally, the nurse managers made assignments, making sure that they were balanced by numbers and the nursing assistants split the units. My new strategy was titled the SOUAR project: **S**taffing **O**ptions **U**sing **A**lternative **R**atios. The essence of the staffing assignments was that some RNs would do primary care and work without the aid of a nursing assistant. Number of patients per RN would be based on severity of illness and the level of nurse experience and proximity of patients; thus, there would be a difference in the ratio of patients. The assistant nurse manager or charge nurse had to arrive to work thirty minutes early to do patient assessment and review report with the ongoing shift to categorize the patient care assignment. Classes and marketing of the concept took almost a year.

I thought the staff was ready, but three months into implementation many of the units were not using the SOUAR method. The project failed because the bar was set too high. Each step in the change should have been gradually added over a period to allow for adaptation. If goals are too high, staff becomes discouraged, and failure ensues rather than achieves the anticipated motivation.

Never wavering in my commitment to build relationships internally and externally, my position was tested. Alvin Junior College invited me to their fiftieth anniversary to represent nursing, and I was flabbergasted. I couldn't believe it. I was torn between "to do or not to do." I told the director that I had not had a great time at Alvin, and she said she was not there at those times and did not know anything about that. I knew and understood that, of course. She explained that my name came up several times as the person to represent nursing.

I reminded myself that participation in this event was a positive for my organization in that it increased its visibility; thus, it was good for me to do it. I gladly accepted the honor. It would be my first trip back to Alvin since 1969.

Ellis, Louise, and I attended the grand affair. Gone were my inferiority feelings and anticipation of humiliation as I entered the room. The administration, board of regents, and other dignitaries' words of appreciation exuded a friendly atmosphere. Attending that event was one of the best decisions that I had made. After all was said and done, Alvin gave me my wings into this exciting nursing career that I was now enjoying.

Having George and Mr. Stein's financial support, I was in a position to create the monthly cultural diversity program. The managers poured their hearts and souls into it. We celebrated different cultures with their food, dress, cultural artifacts, and a program that gave insight to their religion, family and social preferences and habits. It helped all of us to have a higher level of appreciation and respect for each other.

During the Indian Diversity month, Mr. Cunningham volunteered to share his pictures from a recent vacation in India, and it was well received. This program drew the attention of other departments and created interdepartment unity among people of many cultures and backgrounds.

More changes occurred, and my title was upgraded to chief nursing officer to coincide with community titles for nurse leaders. Organizations throughout the medical center were hiring chief nursing officers with doctorates. Magnet status recognition required a master's degree for the chief nurse.

There were discussions as to whether the district needed a chief nurse executive to oversee nursing across the clinics and all of the hospitals, especially in light of the fact we were striving for Magnet status. A lot of pros and cons and rumors abounded. No decision was made. Several people from my community asked me to run for school board again. I had lost two years prior.

I consented to run with the help and direction of Lee, my campaign manager. The many nights, evenings, and weekends spent on the campaign trail, I encountered new and difficult experiences. This was a brutal battle that required new punches and levels of endurance. I learned political skills and more than ever I was steadfast in my beliefs that integrity is the only and best way to achieve a goal. I chose not to use character assassination as a tool of my campaign. After a hard fought battle with Barbra, I scored a knockout and won the election by a wide margin of votes. It was a grueling two-year commitment.

A glutton for learning new processes and taking new risks, this adventure trumped all past challenges. Not being an experienced board member, I was startled as I began to learn the board operations. The monthly board meetings lasted late into the night, wreaked with havoc and disagreements. Fran, the board president who became a good friend, attempted to dignify the meetings, but board members were power-driven. Board decisions were usually split between the group who focused on what was good for the children and those who had ulterior motives.

I gained insight and a broader perspective into many issues impacting children's education that made serving on the board worthwhile, in light of the fact that much of what transpired I could not and did not support. While serving on the board I created a future nursing program between the hospital, my sorority, Zeta Chi Chapter of Chi Eta Phi and Smiley High School that lasted a year. I rode the bus with the fifteen students who were bused to Ben Taub for monthly classes and meetings to learn about nursing.

With the nursing shortage, nursing needs to be a vivid picture in the minds of students so that they can decide early on to make nursing a career choice. The program lasted a year until the schools' superintendent was fired.

Five years later, I was attending a meeting at Prairie View College of Nursing and stepped up to the receptionist desk in the dean's office to ask for directions.

The young guy who responded asked, "Dr. Ashley, do you remember me?"

"No, I do not."

He said, "I'm Brandon. I was in your nursing club from Smiley High School, and now I am in the nursing program here at Prairie View."

"Oh yes, I do." At that moment I could not have been happier had I been told I had won the lottery. I rushed around to the other side of the desk and gave him a big hug. "Congratulations. I had no idea what happened to the kids in that program." As I walked to the conference room where my meeting was, I thought, *If I can influence just one person to join the nursing profession, I am leading.*

At work, we were busy creating a corporate culture when Mr. Guest, the CEO, abruptly threatened the board of managers with his resignation once again. This time they accepted, necessitating another change in senior administration. Mr. Lopez, COO, became the interim CEO, and after some months, he became the CEO. There were several more administrative changes.

The quest for a chief nurse executive resurfaced on the agenda, and finally it was posted. I did not contemplate applying because I was in my dream job and was happy with my success in it. Surprisingly, a couple of people that I would not have expected approached me and encouraged me to apply. There were friends who urged me also. I reviewed the posting and determined I was readily qualified. Experienced in every level of nursing administration, exceeding the education requirements, with long-standing, productive work record, backed by evidence, community recognition awards, and had demonstrated loyalty to the district, more than solidified me as a viable candidate.

Although I had not dreamed of this position, I nudged myself to think about it. This was a great opportunity, so brainstorming began. Kathy, a colleague in the community, called me to express her interest in the job but said she would never apply if I was applying because I deserved that promotion.

After that conversation and with the prodding I got from internal supporters, I got into the ring. I felt no anxiety, butterflies, or anticipatory what-ifs. If selected, this position would be a bonus to my existing joyful career.

After the initial interviews, a long time elapsed, and there was no news, so I scratched it off my waiting list. Unexpectedly, on a Tuesday, Mr. Lopez told me he needed to talk to me and would call me later. I responded, "No problem. I always work late, so feel free to call." Later he called and told me that I had the job. Astonished, I asked for a few days to think about it, and I would give him the answer.

For the next two days, I had to come face-to-face with uprooting my homestead at Ben Taub. My thirty-five year lease was up, and I was contemplating a move. I called Mr. Lopez and accepted the job with the promise that I would not announce it until he had a chance to send out the memo. The next day I was walking down the hallway on the way to the director's meeting when Martha asked, "Is there something you need to tell us?" I said, "No, why?" She said, "I heard you got the position." That jaw-dropping remark startled me. I asked, "Who told you that?" She smiled and said, "I know."

If one director knows something then they all should know the same thing, so I shared with them that Martha discovered I had accepted the chief nurse executive position. I was letting them all know, but it was not to be announced. However, someone went out and spread the word, and by noon it had gotten back to Mr. Lopez. He called and asked why I made the announcement when he asked me to wait until he announced it. I explained it was leaked from his office because I had not told a soul initially but felt compelled to tell the truth when asked; therefore, I shared with the other directors since Martha already knew. He seemed to understand.

After the formal announcement, Pam took charge of the transition from Ben Taub to the administrative complex at Holly Hall. Carla and Pam orchestrated a promotion event and party that was fit for President Obama and more than I could ever imagine. I was aware that it was being planned, but I was not privy to the contents of the program or its overwhelming beauty, which included decorations, food, and heartfelt words of encouragement for me in my new role as chief nurse executive. Carla created a huge poster with my picture and an inscription with From CNOpportunity Ben Taub to Harris County Hospital District CNExellence that was displayed at the reception. Ellis had it framed, and it is hanging in my foyer at home.

Leadership Point

Round Ten

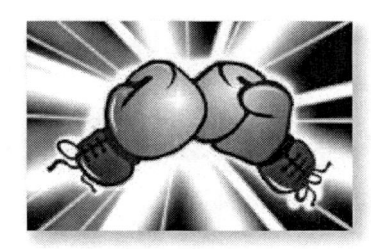

Choose sparring partners that you can learn from

1. Over come shyness and fears and admit your weaknesses.
2. Connect with strong leaders who possess skillful punches.
3. Spend time with your sparring partner discussing and debating strategies to increase your skill.
4. Recognize you can't really know your weaknesses/strengths until they are tested.
5. Visualize success.

CHAPTER 11

Super Heavyweight Champion

AS THE CHIEF nurse executive (CNE), I was responsible for nursing at Ben Taub, Lyndon Baines Johnson, Quentin Mease, twelve community centers, seven school base clinics, and the homeless programs. In addition, I oversaw patient education, quality management, and nursing research. Developing an umbrella for nursing leadership would be the litmus test to bonding with the existing senior leadership of these entities.

Moving to the corporate office, Carla and I both felt fit for the battles. Pam did an outstanding job in getting my office decorated, with Anetta adding extra touches using my personal funds. It was an attractive office and admittedly drew attention. New beginnings, new office, and new office mates translate into adaptation.

David, the CEO, now my boss, was friendly, open, and accessible. He was not a micromanager. As a matter of fact, he told me to sketch out my job description. My first pang of loneliness was missing the directors and all of the Ben Taub employees that I was accustomed to seeing every day. I wondered, *Is this what the empty nest syndrome feels like?* When anyone from Ben Taub came by to say hello, my heart always skipped a beat.

Recognizing that I needed to get to the other sites, I sat with Carla to make a temporary schedule of time to set up individual meetings with thirty people within three months. It was a huge undertaking as getting on to someone's calendar is like trying to get a standby flight. Every week I met and discussed nursing needs and my vision with a clinic director and the chief physician, getting to know them.

The clinics were located throughout the different parts of the city and surrounding areas. Identifying the clinic staff took a lot of effort whereas at LBJ I knew the majority of the managers and leaders. Relationships would need to be developed in small bites.

To compare the chief nursing officers and the chief nurse executive roles, I asked myself the question, *What is the difference between a heavyweight and a super heavyweight boxing champion?* In boxing, the size and the weight determine the difference between the two. Likening the Chief Nursing Officer to the heavy weight and the Chief Nurse Executive to the super weight, the chief nurse executive position is distinguished by the elusive role, fragmentation and massive accountability. The difference warrants an open-minded approach.

First, relationships are long distance because the nature of the work and location of the organization did not permit daily contact with my direct reports who are high-rank leaders. Quality versus quantity is the only method available to establish relationships. As the CNE, I was a coach and coordinator of other leaders. The number of layers placed a distance between me and the directors who reported to the chief nursing officers.

I had positive working relationships with the chief nursing officers, Elizabeth, Barbara, and Michelle who had dual-reporting relationships to me and their respective hospital administrators. I already knew the administrators for the hospitals and clinics, but in my new role, we shared responsibilities with the CNOs. A special skill is required to be effective in achieving goals through dual accountability.

A self-centered or a "my employee" approach can be counterproductive to achieving outcomes. It has to be a united process with each respecting the principles of collaborative leadership. This new experience challenged me, and I was enthusiastically motivated to make it work. It did work, and lines of communication were kept open.

Establishing communication across the spectrum was an experiential task, yet essential to moving forward. Trial and errors were made, but we were off to a great start. I discussed my vision for a Center of Nursing Excellence to link nursing together under one umbrella. The chief nursing officers, research director, and I worked on the components, and then there was a retreat where all of the district directors could work and give their input. A new experience for them as many did not know each other.

A quarterly meeting for nursing leadership was created for chief nursing officers, directors, and myself so that we could accomplish goals and communicate as a team. Not having this type of forum before, the directors from the clinic expressed the benefits and felt inclusive.

The Center for Nursing Excellence would place all of nursing together and provide a focused identity for nursing and a structure from which nurses participate in research and coordinate and facilitate patient-care processes that lead to superior outcomes. The objectives were to:

1. develop a dynamic nursing culture that is embraced and respected, both internally and externally, by facilitators and consumers;
2. enhance professional and collegial relationships among nursing leaders across the district;
3. synchronize best practices throughout the pavilions that lead to excellence in outcomes;
4. provide a framework for becoming a notable organization for nursing research and evidence-based practice;

5. foster excellence in practice and continuity that is recognizable to external constituents.

We had a tangible framework to unite nursing. The next step was to operationalize each objective over the next three years. Considerable time was spent presenting this framework to chief physicians, other administrators, directors, and nurse managers.

Attending other senior-level meetings, I felt my voice was heard, and I was assimilating into the role and revitalizing the senior position of nursing in the district. I had to define the channel for handling or moving issues up the chain of command in that the pavilion CNO is where it starts, not with me. I was careful in how that was communicated with a certain level of employees and physicians so as not to ruffle feathers or to appear uninterested.

As the chief nurse executive, there were no in-house peers whereas the chief nurse officer has peers. The common phrase "It's lonely at the top" could have applied there had I not had a good relationship with the chief nursing officers and other leaders. The new role exposed me to other chiefs in the medical center and other senior-level community meetings.

I received a call to be the keynote speaker for the capping ceremony at Alvin Junior College. I informed the director that I would do it even though I did not necessarily have a lot of fond memories of Alvin. I was eager to sit down and carve out my message from my passion for nursing. Louise accompanied me to the program, and I delivered the following speech.

2005 Speech Alvin Community College

Good evening. I am excited and elated about the opportunity to stand at the podium on this auspicious occasion. To the college administrators, my fellow contemporaries, the families and friends of the graduates, and most importantly the graduates themselves who are the newest addition to the world of professional registered nursing, congratulations on your achievement. I feel honored and privileged to be your speaker this evening.

Someone once said that in any nursing program there are three kinds of students: those who watch things happen, those who wonder what happened, and those who make things happen. Obviously, you have made things happen because we are here tonight to celebrate your graduation after completing a tough nursing curriculum. It is not the man with a motive but the man with a purpose who prevails.

Thirty-seven years ago I was allowed the opportunity to attend Alvin Junior College. The Civil Rights Act of 1964 paved the way for the schools to be integrated, and I was accepted into the nursing program here at Alvin Junior College in 1966.

It was one of the happiest days in my life. However, I will not deny or ignore the fact that I faced challenges related to integration during my matriculation here at Alvin College. At times there were things said and done to me that were insurmountable and often disdainful.

But when you are willing to make the sacrifice and keep your mind on your dream, you can endure the struggle. The father of success is work . . . The mother of achievement is ambition. I testify to that.

One thing I want to confess to you is that I have a passion for nursing. I knew at the age of fifteen that I wanted to be a registered nurse, and I also knew that my family was too poor to send me to college. Nonetheless, I was determined that my dream was not going to be hampered by my situation.

Stephen Covey in his latest book, *The 8 Habits: From Effectiveness to Greatness,* states, "When you are inspired by some great purpose, some extraordinary project, all your thoughts break their bounds. Your mind transcends limitation, your consciousness expands in every direction, and you find yourself in a new, great world."

In 1966 my new and great world was Alvin Junior College. Alvin provided me a break. You see I could live at home in La Marque, Texas, and drive to Alvin every day while holding down a full-time job. Not an ideal situation, but it was the only affordable opportunity for me at that time where I could attain my RN. I was ecstatic and overjoyed. I was about to embark upon my dream to become a nurse. You create your future by what you dream today. I decided that nothing was going to stop me.

As far as I was concerned, my graduation in 1968 was the biggest event in history for me. Now when I reflect upon that time and face reality, I know there were certainly more noteworthy events to remember than my graduation. Lyndon Baines Johnson was president of the United States of America, and Martin Luther King, leader of the civil rights movement, was assassinated. In 1968 my favorite song was by Marvin Gaye, "I Heard it Through the Grapevine" and the Supremes, "Where Did Our Love Go."

All of those memories have historical significance, but my graduation captivated my heart then and still remains the most significant event for me. It was the stepping-stone to my career.

When I attended my pinning ceremony, it was very different than yours. You see I wore my starched cap, stiff white pinafore uniform, white shoes, and hose. That was considered the epitome of how an RN should look. There were no men in the class.

So what was nursing like in 1968? Well, nursing is and always has been a great profession. Having worked through nearly four decades of nursing I have witnessed and taken part in many changes and advancements. I can articulate that nursing once was a profession dominated by physicians; the nurse had limited authority and was viewed as a handmaiden.

When I got my first nursing job, nurses were expected to start on the 11-7 or 3-11 shift prior to earning a 7-3 shift. I made $240 a month and got paid once a month. There was no such thing as staffing ratios. You had to take care of a lot of patients and do the work of the respiratory therapist, physical therapist, sterile supply technician, transportation, dietary, and many other departments. Pharmacy was closed on the 11-7 shift. Often the supervisor became the pharmacist. There were glass syringes, glass IV bottles; beds had to be cranked up manually. Technology was unheard.

HIPPA and JCAHO were not the watchdogs. Patient safety and patient satisfaction were not priority functions, and orientation to the work environments was scarce. Now in 2005, each of these elements are regulated and mandated. We have come a long way.

Nurses were always responsible for the patient but lacked official autonomy to make independent decisions. The nursing process: assessment, planning, implementing, and evaluation, remained a constant.

Over the years, as nursing has moved forward, nurse leaders have stepped up to the plate to ensure that nursing is a leading profession. Nurses are respected. We have authority. We are responsible, and we are accountable for patient care outcomes and nursing practice. Nurses are chief executives, managers, independent practitioners, professors, researchers, etc. We can work in any place where health care services are offered and make a contribution.

Quality and excellence in service is an expectation of all organizations. Organizations cannot achieve this without a sufficient number of RNs. Emphasis is placed on organizations being recognized as Magnet status hospitals, which indicates that the nursing environment is innovative and meets the rigors of excellence in care, service, employee satisfaction, and physician satisfaction.

I recognize that we have a critical nursing shortage, which is in part due to an aging nursing society, a shrinking workforce, and sicker patients. That being said, it is still a great time to be a nurse. Despite modern technology and new nursing and practice models, staff nurses are one of the most important resources in our health care system. Nurses are the backbone of health care organizations and comprise the largest group of the hospital workforce. We must continue to recruit new people into the profession; thus, each of you who walks off this stage this evening must go out and become a recruiter for the profession.

Nurse leaders recognize that the best way to change the perception of the profession is from the inside out. We must retain nurses by creating healthy work environments. The hallmark of an excellent work environment is one that is dynamic, living, breathing, and a constant learning culture of professional nursing practice that challenges tradition and creates new realities for patient care, founded in knowledge and best practices. Nursing environments are moving toward an evidence-based practice where nurses use benchmarks, research, and data to change practice.

As a graduate of Alvin Community College you must be confident that you have been given a basic foundation and sufficient skills to practice nursing. Anxiety is common in new graduates. You may experience stress, transitioning from student to a practicing professional nurse. Moving from a familiar educational environment into the workforce where expectations are that you move rapidly to function as a competent nurse. Nursing environments are equipped to provide coaching, training, and nurturing to assist graduates to excel. We want you to succeed.

Nurses need to be confident more than ever, and that's a good thing. Confidence is not arrogance, conceit, or a sense of always knowing the right answer. When you have confidence, you discover that persistence and hard work yield the best results. You discover your core ideology by looking on the inside. It has to be authentic. You can't fake it. Confidence guides and inspires.

Nurses who are confident will win out most every time over equally talented nurses who are insecure. It is important to feel good about what you have to offer in the health care arena. The combination of knowledge and confidence usually leads to success.

It is imperative that you know that every effort is made to ensure that you transcend from novice to advanced beginner, to proficient to expert.

Much of the forward movement is incumbent upon you. You move from acting like a nurse to coming into your own and being a nurse.

Excellent orientation programs, preceptorships, mentorships, and internships are available at most institutions to assist you in becoming a consummate professional. Continuing learning is a career-long process. I don't want to scare you, but actually you've just begun. Don't throw away your backpacks, library cards, or books; more education is a given.

There is a lot of focus on the BS in nursing as an essential for professional nursing. When I graduated from Alvin, the dean and nursing journals reported that by 1985 the associate degree nurse would become a registered nurse technician. Nineteen eighty-five has come and gone some twenty years ago, and there has been no change.

The fact of the matter is associate degree nurses are needed and are making a viable contribution in health care. Nurses who desire to earn a BSN will find a multiplicity of options to assist you to earn a BS.

Tonight May 5, 2005, is a turning point in your life. You will step out into the world armed with an associate degree, prepared to take the state board of nursing exam to attain your license to practice.

An exciting career awaits you. All you need is a passion for nursing, and you can expect great things to happen. Only passions, great passions can elevate the soul to great things.

I challenge you to do three things:

1. Keep away from people who belittle your ambitions. Small minded people do that, but the really great people make you feel that you too can become great.
2. People who never do anything more than they get paid for never get paid for any more than they do.
And lastly,

3. Say this to yourself. What I perceive . . . determines what I receive . . . which determines how I achieve.

    Congratulations, and I wish you much success.

Receiving a standing ovation, I graciously accepted the accolades and exited the podium to the hallway to get a drink of water where I met some of the attendants who again offered congratulatory remarks. That opportunity to deliver the speech speaks volumes about my mental attitude. I felt good. My emotional freedom from fear of inferiority feelings was severed from the past. Letting go of the past, concentrating on the present, and envisioning the future were my focus. Leadership is not about the moves you make but the attitude toward your commitment.

Achieving Magnet status was now processed as a district goal and required some revamping to revitalize and restore the zest to work collaboratively on it. Restructuring the team with new ideas and recommendations got us on track. We made an assessment and figured out that we were two to three years out, hoping to apply in two years. In the meantime, Texas Nurse Friendly, a new recognition program from the state, emerged. I offered the information to the CNOs, and Ben Taub chose to go after it with Viola being the chair; they achieved the designation.

A strong presence in the health care community is triggered by the organization's visibility in the community. Eager to share employees' accomplishments, I imposed the notion that we nominate our deserving staff for different types of awards. Typically, we had not done a good job of doing that, so I really pounded our publicity department to work with nursing to enhance this goal.

The Performance Improvement Fair was an annual feature at Ben Taub headed by Jimmie. I expanded it to a district affair with all hospitals and most of the clinics participating. It was a spirited means of sharing quality outcomes and another rung on the ladder of unifying nursing. Attendance was high, and awards were given for first-, second-, and third-place winners, and there was a people's choice award. Pride, unity, and success were illuminated throughout the day, especially when the administrators came by to view the presentation and interact with the staff.

Nursing was moving in the right direction, and the team of CNOs was geared up. We passed JCAHO my second year as the CNE. The Patient education department led by Pat was stable and without major issues. They were positioned throughout the organization. Ken the director of nursing research was busy helping nurses to acclimate to conducting nursing research. Several nurses were working on collecting their data for research projects and had presented at research conferences. I felt good about the way the majority of my responsibilities were being orchestrated.

There was one major battle that existed for quality management. Positions had been severely cut, and more were recommended to be cut. Connie and I worked hard using every justifiable data and evidence to establish the need for the positions. They were not removed from the budget nor were they funded. Promises, more meetings, and more discussions led to an impasse.

It was not a mean-spirited battle, and George listened; however, we did not fully convince him of our needs because there were no reliable benchmarks. I had not had an enduring battle of this nature in some years. I did not resolve this issue prior to my retirement. I felt let down and wondered whether a decision consistent with the request would ever be made.

I pondered along the lines spoken by Theodore Roosevelt in a 1925 speech delivered in Sorbonne, Paris:

> It is not the critic who counts; not the man who points out how the strong man stumbles or where the doer of deeds could have done better. The credit belongs to the man who is actually in the arena, whose face

is marred by dust and sweat and blood, who strives valiantly, who err and come up short again and again, because there is no effort without error or shortcoming, but who knows the great enthusiasms, the great devotions, who spends himself for a worthy cause; who, at best, knows, in the end, the triumph of high achievement, and who, at the worst, if he fails at least he fails while daring greatly, so that his place shall never be with those cold and timid souls who knew neither victory nor defeat.[1]

Leadership is also about knowing when the push to change becomes irrefutable and there is a need let go. Rest the issue for now. It took patience and courage for me to recognize that at that time it was my only option. It would be revisited but not then.

Carla entered my office, eyes bugged, with one hand over her mouth, closed the door, and said, "*Advanced Nurses Magazine* just called, and you have been selected as Nurse Leader of the Year." We embraced and expressed our feelings of sheer joy. I commended and thanked Carla for submitting the nomination.

I remembered she worked hard to convince me to let her do it. I thought to myself, *What a great assistant. Most assuredly she is destined for success.* She had completed her BS and was nearly finished with her master's. My regret is that I would not be around to witness her move forward in her career.

Her excitement about me appearing on the front cover of a magazine stirred up the accolades. This was my last hurrah as my retirement was just two months away. Many people across Texas that I had known and had not heard from in years, and even people I did not know, saw the magazine and sent me cards of congratulations.

---

[1] *Theodore Roosevelt "Citizenship in a Republic," Speech at the Sorbonne, Paris, April 23, 1910.*

Gilbert, an RN from Forth Worth whom I had never met, read my highlights and sent me a letter introducing himself and asking me to be his mentor. Of course I responded yes, and I felt like a seed of greatness. What an honorable request from a stranger. We touched bases weekly, sometimes twice a week, by e-mail or phone to discuss management and leadership issues. He came to my retirement where I met him for the first time, and we further bonded and remained friends.

One month prior to my retirement I redistributed my committees, forums, projects and executive meetings among the three chief nursing officers. I aligned the assignments with their interest and strength. They were astonished at the numerous meetings and projects that I had going. I wanted the vision for nursing to be kept alive and active until a chief nurse executive was hired.

January 31, 2006, finally arrived, and there I stood before a huge audience of staff, peers, superiors, community friends, and family. Everything on the program was a surprise, and it was especially warming that the chairman of the hospital board and chief of commissioner's court presented me with a proclamation in person. Other proclamations from the governor, commissioner, and state representatives were read. We witnessed a sensational program, planned and directed by Carla entitled, "The Phenomenal Pearl." Carla wrote and dedicated a poem to me (see appendix 1). Many other inspiring words were written and said (appendix 2 and 3). What a magnificent celebration. I had celebrations before, but my final walk was captive, memorable and left me loving the district as I had loved it for thirty-seven years.

Leadership Point

Round Eleven

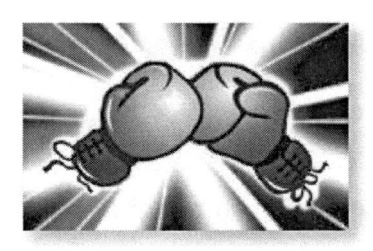

Train, Train, Train until You Retire from the Ring

1. Recognize the need to change punches, styles and techniques.
2. Keep up with new leadership trends through seminars, networking, and reading professional journals etc.
3. Invest in ongoing programs/activities that keep you mentally, spiritually and physically strong.
4. Stay fit for the battle.
5. Balance your attack with the new and what works well for you.

CHAPTER 12

Retirement from the Ring

AFTER THAT HUGE retirement celebration, the limousine dropped my family and I off at my house, and the stark truth engulfed me—my leadership reign was over. Still on an emotional high from the celebration, I felt no emptiness or sadness, just joy because the words of the song, "My Way", by Frank Sinatra sung by Steve at the retirement celebration, reverberated throughout the night. On arising the next morning, at first I thought, *This is my day off.* Then reality hit me, *You are retired.*

I flung back the covers and hopped out of bed as if something had stung me. I was feeling eerie. My inner voice was saying, *How are you going to handle the absence of that emotional stimulation that work gave you? What does this really mean? Where are you headed?*

I was about to find out.

Days turned into weeks, and weeks into months as I dabbled in different things. It was kind of like being at a Chinese buffet where I chose a plate of unknown foods to taste, hoping to determine what I really wanted to eat. It hit me squarely in the middle of my dabbling, *Retirement is not for me.* I now understood why just to name a few, boxers like Muhammad Ali, Sugar

Ray Leonard, and George Foreman, returned to the ring after announcing their retirement and layoff.

They were older, slower, and wiser but craved the need for battle. They attempted a comeback and made a decent stab at it but soon figured their time had come. My inner turmoil was shooting to the surface. *No, no, I cannot dare make that mistake.* Ellis had told me it was now or never. Getting calls from nursing agencies and headhunters offering me interim and full-time positions was an emotional comfort that tempted me to consider a comeback.

One offer in Iowa was quite lucrative, and my son urged me to take it since I so badly missed work. After much deliberation, I declined and decided henceforth and forevermore to put the return-to-work idea where it belonged, out of my mind forever. I reprimanded myself, *You retired to write a book. Now get with it.*

Initially, writing a book did not give the mountaintop experience that work provided. Thankfully, some of my friends do invite me to celebrate nurse's week and other events that keep me tied to the joy of nursing. I increased my involvement in church work and now serve on community boards in addition to staying active in my professional nursing organizations. I speak on leadership topics in the community and universities. I review hospitals who are seeking the Nurse Friendly designation, which is now called the Pathway to Excellence. Editing papers and dissertations without charge is a means of helping others develop writing skills that I find time to do, and the joy experienced is worth it.

One of the things that I really enjoy is helping people to resolve problems, especially novice leaders and those who have little confidence in themselves. Fortunately, friends refer people to me for help and recommendations, and they are not always persons in the health care industry. Each time I speak at a leadership seminar I gain a new mentee or two. Mentoring takes up a large block of my time, and Ellis always asks, "Are you getting paid for this? Because you are always on the phone talking about work issues."

Financial pay, no, but the psychological payout is worth a six-figure check. Fulfillment is something you can't buy. Helping people has always been my greatest source of pride. Having something to give, believing that it is appreciated makes a difference. It is the Academy Award I receive and am still enjoying.

Wherever I go, whether to the grocery store, beauty shop, restaurants, shopping, community events, etc., I run into people who know me from the nursing community. On occasion, when a person says, "You encouraged or motivated me to go back to school or changed my attitude toward work," it fortifies my belief that leaders who give more than required reap unprecedented rewards.

The consistency of my encouragement to others on how to have a successful career is based on three simple practices that I use all the time: (1) Kick buts, (2) KISS, and (3) PUSH. Here is what I mean:

1) Kick out of your thought processes: I would but. I used to but. I did but. Replace buts with I will, I can, and I have.
2) KISS means to Keep Investing in Success Strategies. A career or idea consistently grows based on the strategies you implement. You can't wait for something to happen. You have to make it happen!
3) PUSH means to Persevere Until Success Happens. Don't quit when things don't go as planned. Keep KISSing and kicking buts. Take the risk until something begins to happen.

Evoking and enforcing these principles, coupled with the consistent encouragement from Ina, I finally got focused on writing this book. My passion rose like a tidal wave. Writing it became an exciting battle to conquer. Squeezing in on my time to play Scrabble, my most prized pastime, I became intense in getting my leadership journey into print. That familiar adrenalin rush that I missed so much was back. I was on another hayride, and I hung on to finish.

I encourage you, the reader, to embrace my message in the art of getting up off the canvas. It's often a challenge to get up before the count of ten, but . . . it's the only way to stay alive.

When in doubt, *get up off the canvas!*

LEADERSHIP POINT

ROUND TWELVE

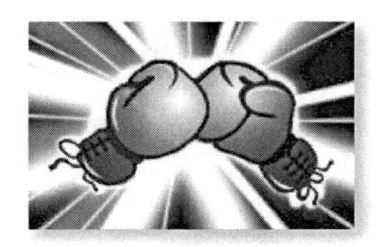

Claim Victory: Win, Lose or Draw

1. Applaud your self when you have given your best.
2. Abandon self defeating thoughts.
3. Recognize that your best is the determinant of a soulful experience.
4. Garner lessons learned from each battle.
5. Hold up your gloved hand in victory.

LEADERS GET UP OFF THE CANVAS

1. Develop a knockout punch.
2. Study your opponent before you get into the ring.
3. Uppercut disappointments.
4. Jab away doubts.
5. Fight one round at a time.
6. Get up off the canvas before the count of ten.
7. Fight with Dignity and Integrity.
8. Produce outcomes that belong in the hall of fame.
9. Become a champion regardless of your rank.
10. Choose sparring partners that you can learn from.
11. Train, train, train until you retire.
12. Claim victory; win lose or draw.

APPENDIX I

Mary Holt Ashley PhD, RN CNAA, BC

The Phenomenal Pearl

THE GASP (SOUND effect) could be heard throughout the exhibit as the crowd beheld the magnificent gem. Its luminescence was captivating; its softness, breathtaking; the uniqueness of its texture-mesmerizing, thus the spectators were left in awe. But despite the apparent admiration of the multitude, none appreciated the beauty as much as the curator who sat quietly in the back of the room. For she knew the history of this pearl; from whence it came, and where it had been. How it was formed and for how long. Intimately acquainted with its growth and development, she cherished every element of its composition.

And rightfully so. For with every tour of spectators, came one who challenged the pearl's authenticity. And today was no different. The boisterous voice came amidst countless accolades "It's not bad, considering. But when you take a cultured pearl that starts with a grain of sand, you can only expect so much. I've seen better."

And as in many times past, the curator clarified the pearl's true origin and priceless value—for this pearl, was like none other. It was phenomenal.

It is this pearl that reminds me of the one for which occasion we celebrate today. The achievements and outstanding accomplishments of Harris County Hospital District's first Chief Nurse Executive.

While many believe true pearls are easily distinguishable, it is imperative that certain distinctions are made. First, there are faux pearls. Worn by those who desire to have a look of originality, they are inexpensive, plastic, and mass-produced, but lack substance. Then there are the cultured pearls, deliberately developed as a result of human intervention. They are harvested, a byproduct of desire for monetary gain and fashionable appeal. But most elite among them all is the natural pearl. For it occurs not at the hand of man, but its creation is divinely and strategically orchestrated, that its integrity will be untainted in all its ways.

You see, many believe that pearls start with sand. But history indicates, this is the least common source. In fact, most pearls start when a wayward irritant enters the intimate flesh of a shell. Its first reaction is to eject it. But when it is unable to do so, it learns to live with it. Its body develops a composite mixture emitting an enchanting light-driven glow known as nacre that begins to coat the irritant, one layer at a time. In the larger pearls, this process is lengthy and occurs slowly. But the hotter the temperature, the quicker the nacre develops.

Nearly four decades ago, there was another phenomenal pearl whose development was soon to begin. But the source of irritation for this pearl was comprehensive. In 1969, this irritant reeked of racial tension and inequities. It was belabored by asthma and chronic long disease. It was replete with financial burdens, and hopes deferred. But the collective irritant that was unable to be ejected at that time, was greeted with a heavy coat of luminescent nacre. When told, "you're not welcome here." there was another coat. When told, "You're not physically capable," there was another coat. When told, "You can't afford it," there was another coat. And when told, "you'll never make it." There was yet another.

And as the intensity of the temperature rose, so did the brilliance of this gem. For the surrounding heat did not mar it. It made it stronger. The irritant intended to destroy, only served as a core of recognition. This pearl came to understand, that not everything in life is desired. Nevertheless, from the undesirable comes discipline and an awareness of what we can endure. At many times, tribulation is divine. For adversity does not build character, it reveals it.

So as the curator of Nursing's phenomenal pearl, let me assure you that she is not enshrouded in plasticity. Her brilliance and brightness are not the result of human manipulation, nor is she driven by greed or aesthetic appeal. Naturally cultivated, she is s a result of divine intervention. The irritants in her life, very much a reality. But in the eyes of those in this room, who admire her most, we recognize that she overcame each obstacle, by sharing her light one layer at a time. In the face of opposition, she shows another layer. When challenged by her circumstances, she shows another layer. When accused by her antagonists, she shows another layer. When struck by despair, yet another.

The brilliance of this pearl is so breathtaking and powerful that it has warranted exhibition in the ethereal realm of Nursing achievement. Touching the lives of both patients and practitioners, we are compelled to celebrate her rich contributions. Pained by her departure in a marriage of nearly 37 years to evidence-based practice and excellence in care, we rightfully honor our treasured jewel, Mary Holt Ashley. From the acceptance of life's hardest blows, to the triumph that set her apart we commend and acknowledge you—as one of Nursing's finest gems.

Carla Brown, 2006

APPENDIX II

A Tribute to
Dr. Mary Holt-Ashley
Chief Nurse Executive
Harris county Hospital District

January 31, 2006 will mark the end of an era for Harris County Hospital District and most significantly the end of an era for our illustrious leader. Dr. Mary Holt-Ashley, Chief Nurse Executive. This day has been proclaimed as the retirement day of Dr. Ashley. Actually it is not "retirement" as we know it. In my humble opinion, Dr. Ashley does not really have the word "retirement" in her vocabulary. Rather it is a term that we use in business and in our society to signify one's separation from their occupation or as Webster defines retire:

> *(1) To withdraw, as for rest, seclusion, or shelter (2) To go to bed (3) To give up business or public life and live on one's income, savings, or pension.*

With these three versions of "retirement", I don't see Dr. Ashley's picture beside either! Mary Holt-Ashley is not withdrawing from anything. She's definitely not going to bed. Dr. Ashley stays up late at night as it is, even with a hard work day facing her at dawn. I can just see her staying up all night, in her mumu, playing scrabble! Her mind never rests—she's always thinking, always working! Mary is not about to give up her business or public life. No, I cannot see that happening! I can't really respond about how or what she's going to live on. This on thing I am confident of, she will live a good life and live comfortably surrounded by family, friends, and colleagues that she has made an indelible print in our lives. As a matter of fact, she is stepping up to yet another level in her well-rounded and exemplary life—to write a book. What a wonderful gift to yourself and to share with others. What a high mark on Maslow's hierarchy of needs—Self-Actualization! This is not to imply that Dr. Ashley is intimating "I've arrived", no quite the contrary, this is Mary Holt-Ashley proclaiming for all to hear—I'm still Growing! Thank you Dr. Ashley, for intertwining your life with mine—for making yourself available, approachable, trustworthy, and lovable. A true friend.

I am a better nurse, a better professional, a better woman, just a better person all around because of knowing YOU! Never stop being YOU!

Written by Viola Hebert, RN, BSN, MA
Chief Retention Officer, BTGH/QMCH
January 11, 2006

APPENDIX III

"Fair Well"

Mary Holt Ashley "thanks for being on the team"
A phrase you used for many years as the First
Executive Nurse on the team

Nursing is not just a job it brings challenges,
excitement, and joy
36 years of your professional service proved you were
dedicated and worked hard

You set major accomplishments showing only the strong
can survive
Advance Nurse Leaders agree that you were the "Best
Nurse Executive of the year 2005"

Personal and professional needs was once part of your
desire
We will miss you, truly miss you and wish you the best
on your retire . . . . Fair Well

Written By: Terrence Lewis
©Copyright of S.E.L.F. ENTERTAINMENT